Read what others h

"You really did it.

You covered most if not all aspects of making a living writing eBooks, from idea conception to writing, editing, compiling, and marketing the finished product.

You don't stop with the marketing techniques that everyone else talks about, you include a LOT of different ways to market, but you forgot one thing, the fluff.

Thanks for all the hard work that I know went into your e-cyclopedia on eBook writing and marketing."

George Wright

"Scott has done what I didn't think was possible! ...the most complete guide I've ever seen. It also covers all of the questions, challenges, and sticking points you'll experience in creating an eBook. No stone has been left unturned in this "eBook Publishing Bible", it condenses years of trial and error, experience, and killer tips into a single reference. Not only is this a step—by—step guide for anyone wanting to create his first eBook, it's also a perfect desk reference for the seasoned veteran."

John Koen

"having been through the product from start to finish, even $67 is a steal. $25.97 is insane..."

Cheryl Lester

This is without a doubt the most comprehensive guide I've read. I was up half the night reading—it's that good. As someone who is in the process if creating my own eBook, I can tell you I'll be referring back to this on a daily basis. ...literally walks someone through step by step, and unlike so many others I've seen, explains each step in great detail, as well as highlighting pitfalls to avoid.

The amount of quality information in this book is astonishing, and I have no doubt that even if a person had absolutely no experience in writing eBooks (and no idea of where to start) he will be a pro by the time he finishes yours. With the amount of information and insight you provide, maybe you should call this an e-cyclopedia. Keep up the good work; I'm off to start writing!"

Andy Robinson

"Wow, I've never seen a book provide as much value as this one. Scott covers every single aspect of the eBook authoring game, including at LEAST 5 - 10 things I hadn't even considered until I read it. He even tells you how to format your word processor, how to choose the right text for your book, and so much more...he's really gone above and beyond... I cannot tell you how valuable this manual is. If you can't use this book to recover the cost of its purchase, then you are in the wrong business!"

Nathan Hangen

"Scott Boyd has written a fantastic and thorough guide to writing and publishing eBooks. It is comfortably laid out for the reader, and offers advice that I have not seen in other publications. I recommend this book to anyone who is serious about their own writing ventures."

Andrea Riffle

"Writes with an informal, friendly, easily understood style that is direct and compelling.

For example, just his "Hot Tips File" idea is huge, relating to any topic you could write an article or eBook on.

Well written, well presented, well thought out... well worth the time and effort to read and study."

Dot Pecson

"To sum up Scott's book, about all I can say is WOW! If you have ever thought about writing your own eBook then this is a must have. Not only does Scott cover every little detail you can imagine, he almost holds your hand as he gives you a step-by-step guide for you to follow. This is hands down the most informative book that I have come across that deals with writing eBooks."

Bryan Zimmerman

"Scott's guide is by far the best guide I've ever read on how to write e-books. He takes you step-by-step and leaves no stone unturned. If you want to know how to successfully write and publish your eBook pick up a copy today."

Jason Bracht

Translators

Make Money Online: Write and Sell EBooks Guide

A Home Business That is Easy to Start

or

Work from Home with an Online Internet Business. Learn How to Make Money Writing, Selling & Publishing EBooks with an Online Home Based Business

Scott Boyd
Globotic Media Publishing
Nova Scotia, Canada

ISBN 978—0—9812653—0—8

10 9 8 7 6 5 4 3 2 1

DISCLAIMER AND/OR LEGAL NOTICES

Author:	Scott Boyd
Proofreaders:	Gerry Boyd
	Sara Boyd

☐

Table of Contents

Introduction:
Why Write EBooks?

Before you get too deep into this information you will want to jump on your computer and go to www.writeandsellebooksguide.com/blog.html. This is where you will receive free updates to this guide and gain access to thousands of dollars worth of video tutorials. You will also receive a 30-day action plan to walk you through your first month in your new business.

People search for all kinds of topics on the internet, but more often than not it all boils down to one thing. Any guesses about what that is?

The answer is <u>information</u>. No matter what topic you are interested in or how much you already know about it; no matter whether you want to buy something or whether you are simply browsing; no matter what you want to know, in the end what you are looking for is quality information.

This is fantastic news if you are looking to earn some extra cash or even carve out a whole new career for yourself online. If you can provide some of the information that people are looking for, you will be rewarded for it, and rewarded well.

That's exactly what this book aims to show you. EBooks are big business, and there is an insatiable market for them that grows daily. Whatever subject you can think of there is probably at least one eBook being sold right now on that very subject. Writing eBooks is one of the most straightforward areas of internet marketing, and the great thing about it is that the more you write and learn, the more sales you will make—until one day you hit on an idea that will sell thousands of copies.

This book aims to get you to that bestseller status quickly and painlessly. It is packed with valuable tips for the beginner, intermediate, and even the advanced internet marketer. You can browse these, or if you are looking for tips about a particular topic, use the Index at the end of this book to make it easier to find specific topics and tips.

Is there really a market for eBooks?

You bet there is. If you look at certain areas of the internet, eBay for example, you might think that eBooks were relegated to history. After all, recent changes in how eBooks are sold on eBay mean that eBooks can no longer be sold as digital download.

Does that mean the eBook is dead?

Far from it. According to Management Practice, Inc. eBook sales in 2007 increased 23.6% over 2006 sales and revenue was up to over $67 million. Even when the eBook is challenged there are still solutions available; for example, you can continue selling by putting the eBook onto CD and mailing it.

But of course it isn't just eBay that generates thousands of sales for eBook sellers every single day. There are countless websites all over the internet that are selling dozens of eBooks. This is a market that shows no signs of letting up or dying out, and the main reason for this is urgency.

In what sense urgency? Well, the world we live in is fast moving and is arguably driven by the internet itself. If we want to find out something, regardless of whether or not it is important, all we have to do is switch on our computers and hop on the net for the answer.

There are eBooks out there on most subjects that you can think of, and that means that with proper research you too can start selling eBooks to serve people's needs in a month or two.

What would you rather do if you knew that someone had the exact information you need? Would you:

- Visit an online book store to order the book you want and wait two or three days for it to arrive.

- Go out to a book store in your local town to find out whether they have a book that serves your purpose.

- Order the book you have just found and be reading it within minutes.

The attraction of that last option is blatantly obvious, and it is that attraction that has sold millions of eBooks in the past, and will continue to do so in the future.

People thrive on getting the right information fast and that is why eBooks are so popular. If you hit the right market and provide the right information you can and will make a good living. And this book will help you to do it.

What are the benefits of writing eBooks?

If you want to build a worthwhile online business then writing eBooks is one of the best ways to achieve your goal. Writing eBooks tends to attract newcomers to internet marketing because it is one of the easiest ways to gain entry into the field.

People read stories about how some eBook seller sat down one day, got an idea, wrote about it and then sold it for $20 or more practically overnight—turning into an internet millionaire. Now that can and does happen, but it doesn't usually happen by accident. Ultra successful people do their homework. They research first and develop a plan to market their product properly. They learn how to take many variables into consideration.

You are about to learn these variables. Every single pitfall, every single stumbling block that could trip you up and prevent you from reaching your destination (a published eBook that sells and sells and sells)... every single one will be covered in this book, so that you can discover how to get on the path which will lead you towards a fantastic income in the weeks, months and years to come.

Here are just some of the benefits you will discover when you write eBooks:

- You can make a name for yourself as an expert on a particular subject. You can easily develop a whole range of related eBooks over time. This is the secret to earning a fortune if you pick the right niche, and you'll find out how to do that very soon!

- You can continue earning money from eBooks you wrote months or years ago. This is called "passive income", since it comes from doing something only once. Once you have several successful eBooks you won't need to write another word again, unless you want to.

- You can use eBooks to help you build a massive mailing list to sell items in the future. This is the secret to making really big money, and we'll look at this in more depth later on.

- You can also earn money by giving your eBooks away for free! Intrigued? Then keep reading to find out how to become a successful eBook writer.

By the end of this eBook you will know exactly what it takes to write and sell an outstanding eBook, and more than that you will know exactly how to write several to start the money rolling in virtually straightaway.

What can you achieve by writing an eBook yourself?

Perhaps a better question would be this one—what do you want to achieve?

There is no limit to what you can achieve with this business. Some people simply use it as a way to enjoy their spare time, making a little extra money on the side. It is certainly a great way to do that, since you can fit this business into your daily routine flexibly. It doesn't matter whether you have a spare half hour a day, or a whole day each week to devote to it, you can always make inroads into this business in one way or another. The secret lies in planning your time— and that will be covered later on in this book.

If you want to retire from your day job and do this full-time, this is certainly an option. Or you can do this part-time allowing you to spend more time doing what you love. For me this includes playing hockey with a great bunch of guys on The Clyde in the AAHL, sitting on my grandparents' deck overlooking the ocean in Cape Breton, spending time having a "small one" (drink of rum) with family and friends, and traveling the world with my wife! It depends on your goals and ambitions, and if you are determined enough to see it through to the end.

So in answer to the question posed at the head of this section, it's up to you to decide what you want to achieve. Only then can you set out to achieve it.

Realm of information products and why you need to enter it

Information products have been popular for years and there are people earning millions from this business, and you can join them. All you need is a strong blueprint to follow, like this one.

It doesn't matter what stage of knowledge you are at. By the time you have finished reading this volume you will know everything you need to know to be able to make your own mark on this million dollar business.

From here on in

What you are about to read is essentially a blueprint for getting that all important first eBook off the ground and available for sale, but do keep it close at hand for future eBooks that you write, because it will help you make the right decisions on what to write, how to write it and who to sell it to. You can always learn more from each eBook that you write, and no matter how much experience you end up with, each successive eBook should get better and better for as long as you choose to carry on writing them.

So, are you ready to get started? Great—then let's get going.

Chapter 1:
The Important Things Good EBooks Have

Here we are at the beginning of our journey to discover how to write a great eBook that will keep on selling indefinitely. There is plenty to learn and discover here, but to begin let's take a look at some of the most important things that good eBooks have.

Let me add that not all eBooks will have every facet included. You may have bought or read eBooks that don't have many, or any, of these at all. An eBook which has all of the following components stands a better chance of selling—and it can be sold in more locations.

Start jotting down ideas for your own eBooks as you work through this book. There is a tremendous amount of information to digest, so start a "Hot Tips" file where you can keep all the nuggets of information that you learn as you are reading. Keeping a "Hot Tips" file is good practice for each informational product that you learn from, so consider breaking the "Hot Tips" document into sections, such as researching niche markets, writing an eBook, recruiting affiliates, and launching a product.

So sit back, find out what the components are, and why they are so important.

A compelling title

This is a biggie. Your book could be absolutely sensational inside, but if the title lets it down you will lose sales. You need a great title, not just a good one. All credit to you if you write an outstanding eBook that is packed with useful content, but you have to convince other people of that same fact, <u>before</u> they buy the eBook.

How to wow readers with the main title

Several things make a good title, including the 'Wow!' factor. It should raise eyebrows and make prospective readers curious. A title that is basic and efficient isn't going to cut it, so think about a best-selling title. Keep these points in mind:

You need to grab your readers' attention because many other e-Books are fighting for it. Try to get prospective readers to read the entire title.

The title must be compelling to hold the potential readers' attention long enough to get them to click on the link or continue reading.

Make the title so intriguing that the reader absolutely must learn more. Bait a hook that can't be ignored.

If you have been researching internet marketing for a while, you know most titles sound the same. Really, they do. Can you remember the names of the last three internet marketing products that you purchased? I can't. They all blend together in my mind, <u>nothing</u> about them sticks in my mind.

Most internet marketers don't consider how their eBook's title sounds. We hammer out information on the computer, rarely speaking our titles aloud until after pre-launch/launch, when it is too late to change the title. Make certain that you choose a title that rolls off the tongue rather than tripping you up.

A great title has to be specific. I could have called this eBook *How to Write EBooks* or *How to Write EBooks That Sell*, but I needed something stronger, and longer, to describe its contents accurately. It also promises a solution for thousands of people looking to make money online. You should include your main keyword phrase in the title, to ensure you get traffic from the search engines when it comes to promoting it later on.

Most bestselling eBooks on the internet have long titles. Some of them are so long you'd have trouble fitting them onto a physical book spine.

Let's suppose you've written am eBook on how to make $1,000 a day online that is absolutely foolproof, very easy to do, and comes packed with tons of proof to show that you have used this method very successfully.

That would be a knock out idea, so you need to have a knock out title. And after some thought, you come up with this...

The Best Way to Make Money Online Today

Hmm. That isn't going to get a lot of attention. It might sound exciting, but it doesn't really say anything. It merely says that you have written an eBook about a way of making money that, in your opinion, is the best.

The title is too vague. Without more information to go on, the reader is likely to skim over that title. Your idea might be the best thing online today, and the secret to how people can make serious money easily, but that isn't evident from the title. Remember, you need to pull people in with your title or there won't be a sale

Start with what you have. What information in your eBook really stands out? What makes it so darn good?

The part that stands out is that number—$1,000 a day. People can remember that. They can see themselves making $5,000 for a five-day work week.

A better title for the above product would be something like this:

The Best Method for Making $1,000 a Day Online

That's more specific. It also makes the point that this eBook is better than anything else out there—and of course once you have hooked people with a great title, you are one step closer to a sale.

Continue thinking about the title while writing the eBook. You will find it is easier to refine over a longer period of time.

How to explode sales with SEO subtitles

A subtitle should be included for the purpose of search engine optimization (SEO). The subtitle should be long and packed with key-words. Thanks to Aaron Sheperd's great book "Aiming At Amazon" I realized that I can utilize my SEO experience to increase eBook sales using subtitles. The subtitle contains your highest priority keywords, with the highest listed first. This is an effective SEO plan for your sales page, back links, and specialty search engines, like Amazon. If you plan to sell on Amazon, this little SEO tip will give you an advantage over most other authors. Few authors know anything about SEO and marketing, so use it to your advantage.

It is important to optimize the subtitle with the exact keyword phrase that buyers are searching for in the search engines or on Amazon or Barnes and Noble. For example, if you are in the golf niche market and you are writing a book about low-cost methods of improving your game you may consider:

> Title: Shave Five Strokes Off Your Golf Score In Five Days
> Subtitle: Make Your Own Putting Green and Practice Your Golf Skills in Your Backyard

This title will appeal to golfers who want to lower their golf score. Perhaps they aren't interested in building a putting green in their back yard, but at least you got their attention. This subtitle is loaded with keywords/phrases that the search engines and Amazon search feature will love. The keywords were selected using the Wordtracker keyword tool.

Although a super long subtitle may seem unprofessional, who cares? The goal is to bring in more sales, and this method works. You are not a college professor trying to impress your students; you are an internet marketer trying to make money. Even when loaded up with keywords, you should be painting a clear picture of what the book is about to your potential buyer. The extra long subtitle actually helps make your title more visible in the search results of search engines and Amazon, which results in more click-throughs.

How long is long? Amazon allows up to 200 characters, including spaces, for the title and subtitle. Lightning Source (more on this later) limits subtitles to 116 characters. If you plan on selling through bookstores other than Amazon, plan on having two subtitles; one for Lightning Source and one for Amazon. Amazon receives new book information from Lightning Source and will automatically upload the subtitle information to create your Amazon book page. To change the subtitle on Amazon you will have to log into your Amazon account and make the change manually.

More tips to optimize your title

The last thing you want your eBook to be is generic. The title has to arouse people's interest, and if it fails many people simply won't read any further.

So you need detail. Let's take a look at some sample titles to see what works and what doesn't:

BAD – How to Save Money on Groceries
GOOD – How to Save 20% Every Week on Groceries

Here we've included an actual amount of money that can be saved. So long as your eBook can prove this, it's a great way of attracting the attention of potential customers.

Here's another example:

BAD – How to Get a Bigger Catch When You Go Fishing
GOOD – How to Reel in a 10—Pounder Before Your Finish Your First Beer

Again, see the difference that a specific fact makes to your title? This would really make people who go fishing sit up and take notice!

Here's one more:

BAD – How to Earn More Money This Year
GOOD – How to Triple Your Income and Work Fewer Hours This Year

Getting the hang of it now? Try this out on your own eBook. Sometimes you might like to plan the content before you pick your final title—you might develop content that reveals a way to earn a specific amount of money or something similar—but you should at least have a rough idea on titles before you get started.

You'll see that I used the 'how to' format in all the above examples; you don't need to do this, but there is an insatiable demand for eBooks that teach you how to do something, whether from scratch or simply how to do it better or in a different way.

When you are brainstorming titles, you need to think about how you search for information yourself online. What would you type into a search engine like Google if you were looking for the kind of information that might be included in our $1,000 a day online example?

My guess is that phrases like 'making money online' or 'internet income' might reel off your fingers and go into that search box. Think of all the possibilities and do some research by using tools like the Google AdWords Keyword Tool (link in the Resources section at the end of this book) to see what popular phrases are relevant to your eBook idea. You can then incorporate one or two of them into your title.

It's worth mentioning here however that while keywords are very important, because they will help your eBook to be found once it hits the internet and is available for sale, they shouldn't make your title clunky or awkward. If it sounds uncomfortable or strange when you say it, tweak it until it works. You can always test it out on a few trusted friends to see what they think of it. After a while though, you will know what works and what doesn't, and the whole process of coming up with a title will become easier.

So a good title is very important when it comes to creating a great eBook. Let's take a look at the other four.

Why you need ISBNs and how to get them

A lot of eBooks are being sold online, and indeed are doing very well, that don't have an ISBN. But, if you take the time to get one for your book, it opens up a whole new world of possibilities.

What exactly is an ISBN number?

ISBN stands for International Standard Book Number. It is a unique 13-digit code that is assigned to each book. There are many benefits to having one.

Many people will tell you that you don't need an ISBN number to sell an eBook, and that is true... in part, at least. You can sell eBooks quite happily without one, but you won't be able to sell them on Amazon, or through any other publisher or book distributor. That's why it pays to get one before you publish the eBook, because at the very least it keeps your options open.

It makes sense to get that ISBN, because the more ways that you can sell your eBooks, the more money you can make. And you can bet your bottom dollar that someone who sees a book with an ISBN number on it will recognize your eBook as a 'real' publication, which is good for your reputation.

The first step to getting an ISBN is to find out which agency you need to contact as determined by where the author lives. The best place to start is www.isbn-international.org/index.html.

Some people are put off by the cost of an ISBN number, which varies by country. You need to consider paying that money up front, or take a chance and publish it without an ISBN number. If it is a success, you could always republish it with an ISBN later. If you can afford to buy 10 ISBNs at one time you will save a lot of money (in the US $270 for 10 compared to $125 for 1).

ISBNs are free in Canada at www.collectionscanada.gc.ca/isn/

Properly publishing your eBook in PDF

PDF (Portable Digital Format) is a way of presenting an eBook so that it looks good and is easy to access, which are the two best reasons for using it. You can do a lot with Microsoft Word, but nothing beats the professional appearance of a PDF document. Most free PDF converts available online will not convert your links, so it is important to use capable software and check your links in the PDF document.

A free option is www.openoffice.org where you can import your Word document, then print to PDF, and your links will work in your finished document. Another option is to use www.cutepdf.com/Products/CutePDF/writer.asp, which is also free.

For print on demand with Lightning Source you will need to convert your Word file to a PostScript file prior to converting to PDF. You can do this for free for 100 conversions at www.e-pdfconverter.com/pdf-creator/pdf-converter/word-to-postscript.html. Click the download link and follow the instructions. Lightning Source requires you to use Adobe Distiller to convert the PostScript file, which is available with Adobe Acrobat Pro, and has a

free   30-day   trial   at
www.adobe.com/products/acrobatpro/tryout.html?promoid=DTELN.
In your Word file click Tools>Options>Save>check the box for Embed
True Type fonts.

1. Save your file.
2. Print to "e-PDF Converter and Creator."
3. Save As a .ps file.
4. Open Adobe Distiller and open the PostScript file you just created.
5. Adobe Distiller will automatically convert it to PDF. Save it in the same folder.

You can confirm your finished PDF has embedded all fonts by opening the PDF file in Adobe Reader then click File>Properties>Fonts. Trust me when I tell you that this alone can save you many hours, or days, of research to find free options that meet the printing requirements.

The beauty of PDF is that almost everyone knows about it. These documents are easy for all your customers to read since most of them will already have Adobe Acrobat—the software needed to open any PDF document.

Make a killing with re-brandable eBooks

If you want to create short re-brandable eBooks (using Viral PDF allows your affiliates to change all the links in an eBook to their affiliate links in seconds) to provide to your affiliates as free giveaways, you will need software such as the free script at www.brandpdf.com or www.viralpdf.com. Don't worry if is confusing. Once you get to this level you will understand the theory behind this powerful affiliate tool.

So stick to PDF—you'll be fine. It is very user-friendly.

Get your own mini-site

What is a mini-site? Aren't all websites are created equal? Well, not exactly. Sometimes having a large website can actually work against you, especially when you want to release a new eBook.

Let's suppose you have your own website which delves into all kinds of things, and you then decide to write an eBook on a subject that isn't related to anything you have on your website.

Once the eBook is complete, you want to tell everyone about it via your own website, but your eBook won't be the focus of your website. In fact, it could be relegated to eBook obscurity very quickly if you don't put it into the limelight.

Why is that? It's because the eBook has to compete with all the other unrelated pages on your website. Even if you give it a page all of its own, it won't attract much attention from the search engine that routinely check your website to see what is new.

If you set up a mini-site that focuses on your new eBook however... well, that's a different story. Everything is zoned in on your book. You can set up a unique domain name that relates to the book itself; ideally this will be the title of the book, so bear this in mind when you are thinking of a good title to use! If you create a great title with keywords, make sure that it hasn't already been registered as a domain name before you try using it for your title. Keep in mind that .com is the most valuable online real estate and has the most world-wide appeal.

Research your keywords and make sure they are carefully integrated throughout the sales page, helping to attract more search engine traffic via the domain name and the content on the page itself.

The best aspect of having a dedicated sales page is that there are no distractions to get in the way of making a sale. When visitors arrive on at your website, they will be reading about your brand new eBook and nothing else. Unique sales page characteristics include:

- No advertising or Google Ads of any kind on the mini-site.

- No links to any other websites—not even other websites that the author owns. An exception to this if you want to trade links with free affiliate directories. You should place these links on your affiliate sign up page where it is out of site of potential buyers.

The entire mini-site is dedicated to making sure that visitors are drawn into your sales page funnel that will lead them to purchase your eBook. Anything that distracts the reader reduces the chance of a sale.

Of course you need to make sure the content on your mini-site is written just as expertly as the eBook itself, especially on the sales page. Luckily for you, there is a whole chapter on the subject of mini-sites included later where we will go into much greater detail.

Something no other eBook has!

What is this special something? Well, I can't tell you that because only you will have the answer, but the best eBooks contain information that cannot be bought anywhere else. If you offer information that no other eBook does you can close the sale more easily.

How do you find this special something?

Begin is by looking at what you are writing about—and if you really want to create something unique, you should do this before you start writing. There is nothing worse than expending great effort to write your eBook, only to discover that your eBook doesn't offer anything new about the subject.

I should point out here that the unique part of your eBook doesn't have to be anything major. If you have made a fortune on the internet and you want to write an eBook about it to help other people, you wouldn't be the first person to do it. But you might have a unique way of doing it, or your eBook may be in a format that hasn't been available before.

By the way, when I say format, I don't mean PDF! What I mean is a step-by-step method of performing tasks that no one else has proposed. You could provide an action plan along with a how-to eBook; it's just another way of providing something different.

Don't worry if you don't come up with something unique right away. Take your time. You will find that you make more sales if you pour more knowledge into each book you write.

Bonus tip to make your eBook scream "read me"!

Another important component is a cover to attract the attention of potential online and bookstore customers.

We spoke about the mini-sites that sell eBooks online a few pages ago. If you decided to buy the eBook, it wouldn't come with that cover; you would simply get a PDF file that you would click on to read.

A professional graphic image can help build credibility by showing the potential customer that you are a professional writer, which results in more sales. Covers may look like rows of open boxes. Others appear to be books stood on end with pages riffled open.

Whatever one you choose, make sure it represents your product well. For example, if your eBook is only going to be twenty pages long you wouldn't select a cover design that looks like a thick hardcover book (spiral or saddle stick designs works better for short eBooks). Never deceive your customers by trying to make the product look bigger than it is.

You don't need to be a whiz at graphic design, and you don't need to get your credit card out to pay for an expensive eBook cover program. Search for free eBook covers using your favorite search engine—and you will find plenty of do-it-yourself freeware.

While the free eBook covers you'll find online are limited (you pay for the software to design something distinctive), many of them could be applied to different types of eBooks. For example, I spotted a good one which depicted a stack of coins; now that could be used for any titles on making money or saving money—maybe even on winning money.

Once again we will be delving into this subject in a little more depth later on, so keep reading to find out all you need to know about getting a great eBook published and sold!

There is nothing worse than seeing a great sales page (the main page of the mini-site where you convince readers to purchase using a sales letter) which has obviously been very well thought out, being convinced that this eBook is for you, buying it... and then being sent a half hearted and very basic book that doesn't do itself justice. The content might be great... but seeing as it doesn't take very long to put something together that really looks the part and is very professional, you'd be missing out if you didn't put in the extra effort.

When it comes to presentation there is a difference between the book that you write and the book that you sell. Now that difference may be very slight—for example, you might only change the typeface and increase the size of the lettering used for headings and subheadings—but even these changes can make all the difference between something that looks like a manuscript and something that looks like a professionally designed eBook. You could also put a border around the edges of each page to keep the eye focused on the information you are giving.

So take time to experiment and make sure the finished product really meets expectations. Some people skip this step, thinking that it doesn't matter because by the time people read what they have to offer they will already have made their sale... but that is missing the point because you presumably want these people to be impressed with your efforts and buy more eBooks from you in the future. Reputation equals future sales in this game.

The moral of this story is that you should make doubly sure that your finished product is as eye-catching and professional as possible.

Will your eBook meet expectations?

Only you can answer this question, but the more effort you put into each stage of the process the better the result will be.

Keep copies of eBooks that you bought from other people close at hand while you are creating your own. You shouldn't copy what the authors of those books have done. You can, however, familiarize yourself with how they have created and presented their products.

And, of course, you should make your eBook better, which will help generate more sales.

I hope that this chapter has helped you identify the components of an eBook. They provide a structure for each section.

So let's move on and look at where good ideas come from... and how to make sure you have one every time you sit down to write!

Chapter 2:
Finding a Best Selling Idea

If there is one thing you need to understand before doing anything else, it is this—all successful eBooks start with a solid idea. The idea provides the foundation for any eBook business, no matter whether you are writing your first eBook or your fiftieth.

Every eBook starts with an idea, but is that idea saleable? Make sure you never get lazy with your ideas, because if you choose one that isn't strong or unique enough for an eBook, then it won't sell.

This chapter focuses on the ideas behind eBooks, because if you get this right everything else will fall into place. That's not to say there isn't still a great deal of work involved with creating an eBook, but you will enjoy the journey far more if you know you have a winning idea in your head!

So let's begin and enjoy.

What do you know?

You will be at an advantage if you know something about your subject, so start by making a list of all the things you know about. This doesn't have to be a job or hobby; for example, you might know about saving a lot of money, or budgeting, or cooking meals for a family of four on $20 a week or something similar. Whatever ideas you get, write them all down. It doesn't matter how weird or crazy some of them might sound; you might be able to alter them or take a different angle on some of them and turn them into winners.

Take your time and keep your list—it probably contains enough ideas to keep you writing eBooks for months!

Another reason why many people stick to what they know—especially the first time—is that it's easier. Why take the time to research something you know nothing about just so that you can try to come across as an expert?

This can backfire because you can end up either getting the information wrong, or simply not being excited about your topic—and that will certainly come through in your writing. There is also a much higher chance that you won't even finish the book because you won't care about what you are writing about, but if you write about something you love, you won't be able to stop!

So stick to your knowledge base and let it do some of the hard work for you. You will also benefit from this knowledge when your eBook is finished and you start promoting it, because you will already know your market and where to find buyers.

Do you have a good idea?

Lots of people write solid eBooks that don't sell. This is where a great writing style isn't enough to make sales for you. If you want to make money from your eBooks, then you need to know how to avoid this.

Good ideas are all around, but that doesn't mean you will make your millions writing about them. You need to select those good ideas that people will pay money to find out more about. You might think that a book on the secrets of celebrity hairdos would be fascinating. However, unless enough other people agree your sales will suffer.

The trick is to pick subjects that appeal to lots of people. Think about this for a moment, because your understanding of this point will make a huge difference to your eventual income. Whatever subject you choose for your eBook, it needs to appeal to one of our basic needs.

What are basic needs? What do we always have an insatiable appetite for?

- Making more money
- Saving money
- Self improvement
- Having better relationships
- Getting a better job or working from home
- Losing weight

34

- Improving our health

All of these examples have one theme in common: they all revolve around us wanting to be, do, or have something better. Virtually everyone will agree with at least two or three points on this list. If you think about it, even people in good relationships want to improve them.

Your eBook must do this for people. If it doesn't, then no matter how well written the eBook, you'll never sell thousands of copies.

So look at your potential idea(s) and see if the topic falls under one of the above bulleted categories. If it doesn't, then you need to rethink your idea(s). If it meets more than one, you could be onto a winner; just make sure though that you aren't trying to cover more than one topic in a single book. This can be very tempting to do, especially for first-time authors.

The moral is this—don't cram everything into that first volume when you can save some of it for future eBooks and future sales! You need to cut it off once you have enough content to over deliver and exceed your buyers' expectations.

A checklist when looking for ideas

Every time you have an idea for a new eBook, run it through the following checklist. If you can answer each question with a resounding 'Yes,' then you have a saleable product on your hands:

- Will it appeal to a reasonably large group of people (i.e. not a tiny niche such as Alaskan eel fishing)?

- Will it solve a problem for whoever reads it?

- Is it different from everything else on that subject at the moment?

These are the three main questions that you need to be able to say yes to. If you can't, then it is back to the drawing board. You won't sell very many copies of an eBook that doesn't do anything for people.

If your idea meets these requirements, then it's time to see if that idea really will fly.

Is your idea saleable?

Don't let that put you off though, because researching potential ideas for eBooks is far from boring! It helps you to determine if your idea will work, and if you need to adjust it to make a real success of it.

And what's more, if this idea is related to an area that fascinates you and has the potential to spawn more than one eBook in the future, you should pay close attention when you do your research.

So let's start researching. A great keyword tool is offered at www.wordtracker.com, and they offer a free trial.

For example, suppose you are thinking of writing an eBook about saving money and budgeting. Enter 'saving money and budgeting' into the Wordtracker 'Full Search' box to see how many times those words were recently searched for by people typing the phrase into search engines. If you only get a few results you might want to think about choosing a different angle or another subject.

A 'Full Search' for the phrase 'save money', returns 1,554 results. But the best thing about this service is that you also get other variations on the term or word you type in. In this case, you'll see lots of other phrases that people have used as search terms as well, which will help you to gauge the popularity of your idea. The most important thing to remember here is that some of the results that appear will be related: so we've got 'save money,' 'ways to save money,' 'how to save money,' and many more which could relate to the topic you have in mind.

You can also use the free Wordtracker GTrends tool at www.wordtracker.com/gtrends to help you out—if you do your keyword search using this page you will see a small graph symbol appearing at the end of each line of search results. Clicking on this will give you a better idea of the search volume of that word or phrase over the past few years. It gives you no more than a glance at the market for your idea and potential eBook, but that can be all you need to determine whether it's worth a shot.

Once you know that your idea is a good one, you can also check what results appear on Google. This will give you an idea of how much competition there will be when you start selling your eBook. You'll need to think about a good title later on, and checking what's in the search engines will help you to choose a title that stands a chance of ranking higher in those results.

Let's look at how our search phrase 'save money' does. As expected, it gets literally millions of results—over 86 million. That's a lot of competition, so make sure that your eBook is focused on a specific area of saving money. This is where your research really comes into its own, because without it you can expect your eBook to compete with millions of other established eBooks.

When researching results for particular key terms on the search engines, look at optimized results for your search term. This might sound complicated, but it's actually quite simple. When you perform a normal search, you simply type the phrase you are looking for into the search box. All you need to do to get an optimized result is to type that same phrase in quotation marks.

When you look up a phrase without the quotation marks, the results you get back will include websites which have most, or all, of the words you searched for, not that exact phrase. If you put the phrase in quotation marks, you will only get the results with that exact phrase. In this case, the phrase "save money" still has over 64 million results, so you would need to zone in on a more precise angle to have a chance of getting seen on the search engines when your eBook finally comes out for sale.

Check out this theory with this phrase on Google 'save money on essentials'. That phrase brings up just over 12 million results on Google, which is considerably better than 86 million. The same search using the phrase in quotes returns 80,000 competing websites.

Tweaking your idea for a hungry market

You may not start with a fully fledged idea for an eBook: you may only start with a vague idea of what you want to write about. For example, writing about how to become a PowerSeller on eBay by selling jewelry is a fully fledged idea, but writing about making money online is a vague one that needs tweaking.

You need to understand that your initial idea may change when you actually sit down to write. For example, you might be thinking that making money by selling secondhand goods online is a great topic to write about, but after researching the keywords, the market, and what people want to know about, you discover that more people are searching for information on how to find reputable wholesalers and dropshippers from whom to buy new stock to sell online.

Always consider the possibility that there could be a better idea out there that is similar but not identical to yours—sometimes you just have to accept that your readers know what they want, and they can be very single-minded about it!

Incidentally, if you stumble over more than one good niche while you are researching your topic, make a note of it—it could be your next eBook.

The power of effective research

History is full of stories about people who bought items to resell because they were sure they were valuable and that there was a market... and those items are gathering dust in basements, garages, and sheds.

There are plenty of stories about people who didn't know whether their idea for an eBook was a good... and then wasted weeks because the market they thought existed for their idea didn't actually exist at all.

At the end of the day, writing any eBook takes time. Constructing a website, buying a domain name and making sure that the presentation and graphics are top-notch, all take time and money. In addition, promoting your eBook can also take more time and much money than you can throw at it.

Furthermore, you will find fruitful areas that you weren't previously aware of, even if you know a lot about the niche you want to write about. You might assume that everyone wants to know about a topic, when in actual fact something completely different might be at the top of everyone's most-wanted list.

The only way to find your niche is through research.

Choosing a niche market

There are many tools available to the aspiring eBook author, but we will only go over the tools that most professional internet marketers use. Most are free or have a free trial that will save you money while you get your first eBook launched and generating revenue.

Wordtracker

Go to Wordtracker and sign up for a free trial. This website is where the professionals do much of their keyword research. I will describe the methods that I use, but you should try several methods to find what works best for you. Perform Full Keyword searches in Wordtracker for each of the topics on your list by following the ten steps below:

1. Log into Wordtracker.

2. Click on "Full Search."

3. Add your keyword or phrase.

4. Check the box for as many of the associated search terms as you wish.

5. Click "Email Results" to yourself and save the email in a "Keyword" file that may be used later, perhaps after your

Wordtracker subscription has expired. Use the keyword that you did the search for as the subject for the email, so that you will know which is which in your email account. The keywords and analysis can be a valuable brainstorming tool when you need to come up with new products for niche markets.

6. Click on "Click for Results" at the bottom of page.

7. Click on all the keyphrases that meet your popularity requirements. Count: This number indicates how many times a certain keyword appears in the Wordtracker database. The Wordtracker database holds about 300,000,000 words, so a count of 200 means that the keyword appeared 200 times in the previous 130 days. Predict: This number indicates the maximum predicted daily searches for all major search engines and directories.

8. Click the "Click Here to Perform a Competition Search" icon.

9. Choose one or two search engines to analyze. The program only allows two search engines for each search to avoid overloading servers. Select Google and the second search engine of your choice. (I usually use Yahoo.)

10. Look for keywords and phrases that could be used for your product. How many keywords and phrases have a KEI (Keyword Effectiveness Index) of more than 100? If there are only a few, then it may be a tough market to break into. The more keywords and phrases with little competition allows you and your affiliates to create articles and blog postings that can rank high in search engines, resulting in more traffic/sales.

KEI (Keyword Effectiveness Index): The higher the KEI number the better. Higher KEI keywords are popular and have less competition. This is a good tool for determining niche markets, domain names, and keywords for webpages.

In this example the results are for Google only, which is about 68% of the market share.

The Competing column shows the results of the number of competing webpages for this search engine. It is a good idea to check out the top search results for the keywords you are considering if the webpages have evidence of advanced search engine optimization (SEO). If the top couple of pages of results are filled with well-optimized webpages, your chance of obtaining organic (free) search traffic is slim.

Search engines

Many people use search engines to find products they want to purchase. Most search engines have pay-per-click (PPC) ads displayed along with the search results. Do a search for the niche market product you are considering. Find out how many advertisers have ads running (PPC) by scrolling down the page. If there are ads all the way to the bottom, click on the second page of search results and repeat until no more ads are displayed. The more search pages with PPC ads, the more profitable that niche may be since it costs money to run those ads.

If you have a Google AdWords account, you can easily see how profitable a niche may be by checking the cost of the keywords for your niche. The higher the cost for each keyword click, the more profitable the niche market is likely to be. This has drawbacks, however; as your affiliates will pay more for advertising.

ClickBank

According to ClickBank, "ClickBank is the online retail outlet for 10,000 digital product publishers and their 100,000 active affiliates. We've paid our clients on time, every time, for 10 years. Over $1 billion thus far. Now with weekly payouts!" ClickBank is one of the topic networks for publishers and affiliates. I use ClickBank for my published products, and it is a great tool for planning your next product.

Go to www.clickbank.com and look in the Marketplace (top of page navigation bar) and search the topics you are considering. The default "Sort By" is Popularity, but you want to change this to Gravity. The Gravity calculation is not published, but the higher the number, the more affiliates are making sales. ClickBank's definition of Gravity is "Number of distinct affiliates who earned a commission by referring a paying customer to the publisher's products. This is a weighted sum and not an actual total. For each affiliate paid in the last 8 weeks we add an amount between 0.1 and 1.0 to the total. The more recent the last referral, the higher the value added."

(For a very detailed explanation of Gravity, check out the following YouTube video: www.youtube.com/watch?v=zvqCB5rr6uo.)

Look for products found on the first couple of pages in Click-Bank's search result listings with a low refund rate and high referral percentage. You can determine a product's refund rate by looking at a products sale price (you may need to click on the link and go to the sales page) and look at the "Earned Per Sale" amount. The difference is due to ClickBank subtracting refunds and chargebacks.

A product with a sales price of $39.00 and a 75% commission looks like this:

ClickBank Fee (7.5% of purchase price + $1) = $3.93
Sale Price ($39) - ClickBank Fee ($3.93) = $35.07
Affiliate Commission ($35.07 * 0.75) = $26.30

If the "Earned Per Sale" for the above product is $23.45, then the refund and chargeback rate can be calculated as:

Affiliate Commission - Earned Per Sale = $2.85
Refund Rate = $2.85/$26.30 * 100 = 10.8%

So the refund/chargeback rate for this product is 10.8%. This is subject to the publisher promoting only one product with this account. The numbers will be skewed if the publisher promotes more than one product with more than one sales price.

However, if a product is on the first couple of pages (e.g., high in popularity), but the gravity is low, it means that not very many affili-ates are making sales... it's possible that just a couple of "super affiliates" are responsible for all the sales. This does not mean you should avoid the product; just understand that if you sell the product, you'll be going head-to-head with people who really know affiliate marketing.

Amazon

Amazon has a wealth of information readily available for the savvy researcher. Use Amazon to see how the books in your niche areas are performing. The following tips will help you determine the viability of a niche for an eBook, print book, or both. Tips include:

- Reading the reviews of the top selling books in your niche (Amazon Rank of 1 is the top seller and a rank of 5,000,000 rarely ever sells). Reviewers often provide valuable information on how to improve the books that you may have read; you may be able to incorporate into your own eBook.

- Using the "Search Inside This Book" tool when possible to see how long it is, and the quality of the information that is provided. If the niche topic or book title is *How To Make Money On eBay,* it is often interesting to see how much of the book is truly dedicated to making money on eBay. A third of the book may explain how to start a business with the same info that is in thousands of other books. If all books on this topic only dedicate a small amount of the content on how to make money on eBay, then perhaps there is a market for a concise and highly targeted guide. I was looking for a niche topic for writing a report and decided to buy a book on the topic, but guess what? No books went into any detail on exactly how to find a niche topic. There are eBooks with a page of good information here and there, but not one complete eBook. So, I found my niche because I knew from looking at internet marketing forums that many people were looking for help on this exact topic. Demand + no supply = my report.

- Buying the books that receive positive reviews and sell well. This method will give you a good feel for the quality of your competition.

- Using the Amazon search feature to determine the amount of competition, the quality of the competition, and the demand for your product.

  - Competition:

    - How many books are being sold that are on your subject?

    - How many books were published on the subject in the past year?

    - Do the quality books from a few years ago still sell well?

    - How many pages are in the book? If all the best selling books on your topic are 200+ pages and you are only looking to create an 80 page book, then perhaps another niche is better suited for you.

  - Quality of Competition:

    - Do the titles and subtitles include lots of appropriate keywords?

    - Are the authors considered experts in their fields?

    - Are there many books highly rated (which will make the field tough to break into) or is there a need for a quality book on the topic?

  - Demand:

    - Are there at least two or three books with an Amazon Rank of less than 5,000? If so, there is likely good demand. Check out www.fonerbooks.com/surfing.htm for

information on how to understand the Amazon Rank
and what volumes correlate to Rank

Forums

Forums are a valuable source of information if used properly. If
you are considering a niche in the golf market, you would do a search
for golf forums and look to see what people are looking and asking for.
Are many people asking for tips on any aspect of golf? Are people asking for advice (think reviews) on putters? Utilize the forum search feature with the following search text:

- "how do I"

- "what is/are the"

- "what do you think/recommend"

I think you get the idea. If many people are searching for the
same information, you have a potential market. Pay attention to the
longest threads as these topics created the most interest.

Consider what markets affiliates promote. You don't want to find
the ultimate niche market only to find out that very few affiliates have
websites, blogs, email lists, or the desire to promote it. Spend some
time looking at affiliate forums to see who is promoting what. Pay attention to senior members that make informative posts and to the
products they are promoting. Forums to check out include:

- www.clickbanksuccessforum.com/forum

- www.warriorforum.com

- www.affiliate-marketing-forums.5staraffiliateprograms.com

- www.jvnotifypro.com

- www.forums.digitalpoint.com/forumdisplay.php?f=87

You may want to spend time reviewing ClickBank product trends in www.cb-analytics.com and www.cbtrends.com.

PayPal

At www.paypal.com visit the Shops by clicking on the icon at the bottom of the homepage. To search the thousands of websites, use the Categories column to look at websites that are related to the product that you are considering. The categories are listed by number of sales (paid for using PayPal). Products that sell well obviously have a market and perhaps there is room for you in the niche.

At eBay do a search for a product that you are considering selling. The search results will state how many items are available in that particular category. This search result is only an indication of how many vendors are offering similar products, not the volume of revenue generated. You can also check on the hot trends for each category at www.pulse.ebay.com.

Surveys

It is very easy to conduct an online survey to determine if you have a viable business or product; the majority of online businesses don't take advantage of this valuable tool. The internet provides immediate feedback, and surveys are used to capture that info in real time. Answers that a survey of your target market can provide include:

- The sales price

- The product's must-haves

- The viability of the product

- The future products or bonus products

Surveys are very inexpensive and some are free! One way to conduct a free survey is to do a search for forums related to your product and post quality questions such as:

- I am considering purchasing a widget, and I was wondering where you buy your widgets.

- I am considering purchasing a premium quality widget, but I am not sure what price range that should be in. How much you have paid for premium widgets?

If you genuinely appear to need assistance, you will receive plenty of responses containing helpful information.

A faster method is to send a survey to the target audience with questions about your potential product. This method is very easy if you use one of the many survey services online. Many providers offer this service for free.

A highly targeted strategy is to use surveys to conduct exact questions that you would like to ask a targeted market. There are survey providers that offer free and paid services such as:

- www.surveymonkey.com

- www.surveypro.com

- www.supersurvey.com

- info.zoomerang.com

- www.surveyconsole.com

- www.inquisite.com

- www.surveysite.com

- www.freeonlinesurveys

If you have your own website, you can ask your visitors to fill in a brief survey and direct them to your survey on the survey providers URL.

A market survey's primary objective is to uncover a potential customer base for a new product or service. If properly crafted, surveys can provide a very comprehensive understanding of your target market. This wealth of information allows you to make a smart decision about what niche market to create a product for.

The following steps will assist you in creating your first market survey:

Create the Survey

- KIS - Keep It Simple:
  - Three to five questions
  - Easy to understand and short questions
  - No double-barrelled questions
  - No open-ended questions
  - Be specific
  - Refine the questions to make certain that you will receive the information that you need or are measuring
  - Test the survey with a small audience to make certain that it works properly and provides the data you are expecting

Sample questions include:

- What would you most likely purchase in the next three months?
- How much would you consider spending on...?
- Questions to Ask:
  - Demographics:
    - Demographic data identifies the potential market with variables including age, gender, race, income, education and location.
  - Factual:
    - Questions that relate to a person's previous experience and yes or no questions.

- Questions that provide ranges rather than specific numbers.

- ○ Attitude:

  - Questions that use a scale that is used to rate feelings and emotions of the survey taker including likes/dislikes, and level of importance.

- ○ Open Ended:

  - Open-ended questions prompt comments and input.

  - These should be used only when necessary and placed at the end of the survey because the answers are hard to analyze.

Additional niche marketing strategies

Pick a niche that can be added to, with at least 10 more topics and can include multiple products such as software, videos, and eBooks. Chances are that it will take many product launches to bring decent checks, so why not use Product #1 infrastructure to make Products #2 - #10 easier and less costly to prepare. Not to mention that you will be collecting email lists of people who will be interested in your related products. You will have three email lists:

1. Affiliates - You have an existing relationship with your affiliates and it is important to continue to provide them with additional products to promote in the same niche. If you offer affiliate tools, then I recommend that you require affiliates to sign up with their name and email address for inclusion in your email marketing program.

2. Customers - You also have an existing relationship with your customers. You should also be providing your customers with a monthly newsletter where you can promote future related products for free. Customers will have to sign up to your "Customers" email marketing list.

3. Potential Customers - You should attempt to capture the name and email address of people who decide not to buy and are clicking away from your mini-site. You can do this using an exit pop-up window that offers a free special report or eBook (something of value that shows the quality of your core product).

Another huge advantage of creating products for the same niche is that you can cross-promote all of them, which will also reduce your time to market and cost. This can also work for niches that are too small for a single product, but can be profitable through multiple offerings. Cross promotion examples:

- Product #3 is the core product and Product #2 is offered as an upsell to generate additional revenue and Product #1 is offered as a bonus or as a part of the core package with Product #3 for a higher price.

- Product #6 is the core product selling for $24.95 and the upsell is Products #1 - #5 bundled for $67.95.

- An example of a niche market with future related products follows:

  - Product #1: Learn to Play Golf Guidebook.

  - Product #2: Drive 300 Yards Straight Every Time Video.

  - Product #3: Special Report: Secret Practice Strategies to Shave 3 Stokes Off Your Score.

  - Product #4: How to Achieve the Perfect Swing Manual/Video.

Once you have launched your first eBook, the entire process for the next eBook will be much faster, which is very important. If you are like me, you need to make enough money to put food on the table and pay the bills ASAP! This likely won't happen right away with the first product, so let's get a system in place to create many products that will each generate at least $500 per month. Once you have saturated the market with products for a specific niche, then you can move onto a new one.

The importance of taking your time

I'm sure you can see why it is important to carefully research keywords during the planning stage. If you neglect this, you could find yourself halfway through writing a 50-page eBook only to find that no market exists for your topic.

By identifying an audience for your product and determining what these people want to know, you are one step closer to solving a problem for them.

Remember that when you are researching a new eBook idea—ask yourself if it will solve a problem a particular group of people have. Will it make it easier for them to earn more money? Will your eBook enable them to win at job interviews? Will they be able to play better tennis once?

You should be sure the idea is strong enough to sustain an eBook. While it's true that eBooks come in different lengths—most of them fall somewhere between around thirty pages up to one hundred—it could be that your idea only warrants an eBook ten pages long.

If that is the case, don't automatically ditch your idea because it could provide a useful additional report you can offer for free to anyone who buys your main eBook (which should be on a very similar subject, and could be suggested to you by all that lovely research you have been doing!).

Is your idea timely—or evergreen?

Timely or evergreen? What's the difference and why does it matter? Let's take a look because it is very important to understand the difference.

TIMELY – a timely idea is an idea that is relevant at the moment. It may be related to an event, time of the year, or something specific to a time or a situation. After that time or situation passes, any eBooks related to it will cease to sell. For example, selling Christmas trees during the summer.

EVERGREEN – an evergreen idea is one that will always be popular. For example, everyone will always want to know how to make more money. An evergreen idea could be popular any time of the year, and in any kind of climate—although it may still have peaks and valleys that happen naturally with any product.

If you had to choose between the two types, which one would you choose? I guarantee that without even thinking about it you have thought or said out loud the word 'evergreen'.

That's the correct answer!

Before I get letters saying that it is possible to make truck loads of money during Christmas season by selling products (and eBooks) that are related to Christmas, let me make it absolutely clear that I'm not saying you cannot and should not use timely ideas as well. Indeed, if you hit the market at just the right time, you can make a great profit.

But there is a lot more work involved in creating timely products and the risks are higher. If you don't hit the market right, or you don't time your launch right, or you get any one of a number of things wrong then you won't succeed.

A timely idea also means that you have to stick to a strict timetable to launch your eBook at the right time. For example, you hired a graphic designer to create the eBook cover, and something happens that results in a delay your schedule can be pushed back several days or weeks. That could result in the prime launch period—and potential sales have disappeared.

If you have an evergreen idea a delay is less catastrophic. Let's look at an example of how a delay will affect an evergreen idea.

If the same delay with the graphic designer happened with this eBook as with the timely idea, what difference would it make to the finished result? If you had a firm launch date planned, that date may have to be pushed back, but it wouldn't affect the volume of sales you receive as a result, since there isn't a prime selling period that you would need to fit into.

It could be more of an issue if you promote your eBook before it is launched. This is a common practice for eBooks; authors announce that their product will be released on a specific date, and the clock starts ticking down to the release date.

If executed effectively, you can have buyers waiting to order the eBook as soon as it is released. The risk is a delay can damage your credibility.

So what is the solution here?

An option is to only announce the release when you have all elements in place. For example, you would make sure that all the following are done:

- You have written and edited the eBook in full, including proofreading and reviews from experts on the subject.

- You have acquired the domain name for your website.

- You have created the website and tested it to make sure the payment link is working.

- You have completed the affiliate's member area complete with plenty of tools to assist affiliates market your eBook.

If you experience a delay with an eBook that is based on an evergreen idea, it won't affect you much unless you have already informed people of the launch date. And as we have seen above, there is a way around that if needed.

Are there downsides to an evergreen idea?

There is one, and it might not seem to be a big issue early on, but you will quickly realize that it can wipe out your potential profits—along with your budding career as an eBook author.

What is the downside? It's procrastination. The only thing you should procrastinate is dying.

If you suffer from this malady already, you're not alone. Procrastination robs you of the ability to get things done. This means no published eBooks to your name if you don't conquer this enemy defending against your financial success.

Let's say you have a great idea for an eBook—one that fills you with excitement and enthusiasm. "Great!" you think. "I can't wait to write this eBook!"

You might even sit down that day and start creating an outline various chapters in your book.

A couple of days later you get started with writing a chapter. You are still feeling enthused and you stay awake at night thinking about all the sales you will make. Before you know it you have several pages written.

Then the enthusiasm and excitement starts to wear off. You realize that although you well into the writing process you have a long way to go to "the End", and it can seem to high a hill to climb.

What usually happens? You put your eBook aside and start doing something else instead, like marketing another author's eBook. You're not going to abandon it; you're just going to give yourself a break, so that you can do something else and then come back to it with a fresh eye again. Don't fall into this trap. I have about 10 unwritten eBooks in various stages of development thanks to this trap.

Stick to the plan, become a publisher, and let hundreds or thousands of affiliates market your eBook!

There are times when a deadline helps to keep you on task. The urgency is responsible for getting that eBook finished and on the market. If that urgency isn't there the whole project can disappear.

Read Chapter Five for advice on how to make sure procrastination doesn't trap you!

While having a timely idea can sell plenty of eBooks, as a beginner you will have an easier journey if you choose an evergreen idea. Work your way through this chapter each time you get a new idea and make sure it meets your expectations before you continue writing your eBook.

One final point before we leave this chapter for new and uncharted territory. It can be tempting to skip ahead and read chapters out of order when you get a new book like this one. That's understandable because you want to know how the whole process works.

But I would strongly encourage you to read everything in the order that it is written, because it is put together to provide you with a step-by-step guide where each section builds on the previous section.

Chapter 3:
Turning That Idea into an EBook

No, it's not quite time to start writing yet. First of all we need to get a proper structure in place.

This is a lot like the researching part of the process. It might seem a bit dull compared to actually writing the eBook and getting it on the market, but by taking the time to prepare a solid structure before you start writing, there is little danger of 'writing yourself into a corner.' This can easily happen if you don't get your thoughts and ideas in order before you start.

How do we build a good structure?

The best place to start is by thinking about what your eBook is going to be about and seeing if you can break that down into chunks. Don't worry about the number of chunks you end up with—there is no magic number. You might have five or you may even have twenty. It doesn't matter, as long as your chunks cover the subject adequately.

You will often find that several areas will be obvious from the title and subject of your eBook. For example, an eBook about saving money could include sections on saving money on groceries, saving money on clothes, saving money on telephone and cell phones, and so on. Alternatively, you could break that subject down and write a separate eBook on each topic (remember what we learned about niches and making sure you are aiming the eBook at a specific audience?) An eBook on internet marketing might have a number of chapters each focusing on areas of opportunities. No matter what your eBook is about, some of the sections will naturally fall into place and this is always how you should start.

Once you have jotted down all the ideas for topics which would form part of your eBook, take a look at them and work out whether or not there is any particular order they should go in. If we take this book as an example, you will see that after a short introduction, I tackle the subject of ideas first. Then comes the section on creating your eBook, then a look at what else you need to provide to create a complete package, and finally the topic of promoting and selling your eBook. To help you visualize you can use an outline with subtitles, which will look like the index.

It would be confusing if I started this book by telling you how you can sell the eBook you have written. You'd be sitting there wondering "What eBook? I haven't even written one yet! I thought this book was supposed to tell me about writing them."

That's why a common sense and well ordered plan of action is necessary to help you break your idea down into sections that are manageable for you to write, and also manageable for the reader to read—and will the reader smoothly through your eBook from the beginning to the end.

Fleshing out the structure

Once you know what sections you are going to have in your eBook, it's time to figure out what needs to go in each one.

There are several ways to do this, but the best is to begin with is to repeat the process you just went through and work out how each section will be structured.

Don't be worried about the process of building structure—it's actually your best friend! What we're doing is breaking down your eBook into progressively smaller chunks, so that when you actually start to write it (which can be a little scary the first time you sit down to do it), you won't be faced with a monster of an eBook that needs to be written. Instead, you'll be looking at bite-sized pieces of information that need to be written. This isn't nearly as daunting and you'll be able to tick each individual one off your list, or outline, as you write. And believe me, that's a great feeling!

Think about it for a moment. Which action would you prefer:

- Sit down with the thought that you have a whole eBook to write? Or

- Sit down with the task of writing a single chapter of that eBook? Or

- Sit down to write one section of one chapter, which may not amount to more than a single page?

I know which one I would choose, which is exactly why I always write eBooks that way.

An example of fleshing out a particular section can be seen by looking at what I did when I made notes for writing this chapter:

Chapter Three – Turning that idea into an eBook

- Getting a structure together

- Fleshing out your structure

- Do you have enough material

- How many pages

- Images or no images

- Benefits and drawbacks

- How is it going to look? (Cover, font, copyright page, and so on)

These are very basic notes, and I had a sheet of 8 ½" x 11" paper on which I scribbled down ideas that came to me that I wanted to include while I was writing the eBook. Well, now you've read my plan for this chapter so you know what's coming next, right?

Do you have enough material?

Once you have your basic structure, it is tempting to start writing right away, but there is one more thing you should check first.

It is almost certain that you will have to do some research for writing your eBook. If you are writing about something you do every day and you know the subject inside out, the only research you may have to do is the checking of specific figures or resources that you want to give to your readers.

If you are only vaguely familiar with the subject, then you will need to do more research to gather enough material. The point is that you should look through your structure as you have it written down and work out whether there is enough there to write your eBook.

It may be that one or two chapters stand out as being a lot shorter than all the rest; if this is the case, have you fleshed them out enough? Are there aspects of those particular topics that you haven't actually covered in enough detail? If you were reading an eBook on that subject, what would you want to know?

By doing this now, you will avoid hitting a block during writing or struggling to figure out how to avoid having too short an eBook.

If you can't find a way past a particular point in your structure, use the internet to do some research on that topic. I have done this in the past and it is quite amazing how many times you will visit a website and read an article that will trigger another idea or some other aspect of the topic that you had completely forgotten about.

Never forget the power of the internet for helping you with material, but always remember that you cannot copy the work of anyone else because that constitutes plagiarism. The idea is to jot down ideas and information that you find online (and in other sources as well, such as books and magazines) and then work it into your own words, so that you come up with something totally unique.

And you will usually find that you can inject your own thoughts into the information you have as well, so that your own voice starts to make itself known through your writing—and that will give you some great results you can be proud of!

Tip – if you find you have a couple of chapters that are very short, combine them with another chapter on either side of them. This doesn't always work, but quite often a part of your topic which is extremely short is that way because it is in a place which is unnatural for it. So think about whether this could be the case, and don't be afraid to edit your structure as necessary—it's a lot easier to do this before you actually start writing!

Finding content ideas

Once you know your niche market you will need to create enough content for your eBook. Hopefully much of that content exists in your head already, but if you need more content there are many great tools that you can use to help you.

EZineArticles ~~Transcatory~~

Go to www.ezinearticles.com and type in your keywords in the search box and review the articles that are returned at the top of the search results. Look at the keywords that the article is targeting and also what the article content is. What is the problem that the article is providing a solution to? At the bottom of the article EZineArticles will list the top viewed articles in the category most related to your keyword that you searched for. These articles should be reviewed and analyzed as they are obviously providing readers with the information readers are looking for. Make a list of the topics covered and from that list you can create an index of topics in high demand by consumers. You can also check out the level of competition by reviewing the websites where the author is linking to in the resource box.

Yahoo Answers

Go to Yahoo Answers and search for questions using your keywords. Take note of the questions/needs/problems people are looking for a solution to. This is a great way to refine your understanding of the problem that you will need to solve to generate sales. Make a note of the questions your market is asking as these will provide you with topics for the articles that you will write about and submit to article directories after the launch of your eBook.

Forums

Do a search using your favorite search engine for forums related to your eBook topic and take notice of the most popular forum topics and threads. Consider including information in your eBook to appeal to these forum posters. Investigate the longest threads with the most passionate responses. This is where you can find a ton of content ideas to attract a large market of buyers. If your topic is technical, you can find many gems of information that would add great value to your eBook. Many people that buy your book will be pleased with the purchase if they find a few nuggets of information that help them.

Amazon

Go to Amazon and research the topic selling books on your topic. Use the "Look Inside" feature to scan the index to get a feel for the content provided in the book. You can also purchase the books to enhance your knowledge of the topic before you start writing. The more you know about a topic the easier the words flow while typing. If you already wrote your eBook, you can still add nuggets of information learned at a later date.

ClickBank

Purchase the best selling products related to your topic at www.clickbank.com and review their content. This is your competition, and if you aren't a big name internet marketer, your goal is to provide a better and more valuable product. Offering a better product than the leaders will give you an opportunity to break into internet marketing quickly by building a reputation for quality products, which can lead to many affiliates and joint venture partners.

How many pages?

There is no real answer to this question, other than to say that each topic and each eBook will be different, depending on how in-depth the subject is.

Generally, eBooks aren't as long as traditionally published paperback and hardback books, but that doesn't mean they are any less valuable. Some topics require more pages to cover the content extensively. In fact the selling price of many eBooks far exceeds the price you will find on the cover of many traditional books.

There are some outstanding eBooks that retail from $19 upwards (and much more), that contain as few as 15 to 20 pages. There are also eBooks which go well over 100 pages and retail for $39, $49, $99 and more. These examples may represent really good value because the information contained in them is often aimed at such a niche audience that the traditional publishers wouldn't be interested in it anyway.

The secret is to make sure you only have the number of pages you need—no more and no less. Don't start worrying if you find your first eBook is only 15 pages long. You can still sell it if the content and sales page are high quality. Content will always be the most important consideration. Don't try to write more than you need to, because you run the risk of weakening the eBook. As you adequately cover everything you need to within the outline of your eBook, that's all you need to do.

A couple more pointers—first, don't limit yourself to a specific number of pages before you start. It can be a good idea to estimate how many pages each section will be as a rough guide, but don't worry if you end up writing a lot more or a lot less. The material will tell you how long it needs to be.

If your eBook ends up significantly shorter than you expected it would be, read through it to see whether you have written down everything you wanted to write initially. Did you miss any sections in your structure? Did you just skim over a couple of sections without really including everything that needed to be said? And did you tell your readers everything they needed to know while you were writing? Is your writing conveying the information clearly?

We will dig into the editing process in much more depth in Chapter Six, but for now you should be aware that you will need to edit your eBook to make it the best that it can possibly be, so don't worry if your first draft doesn't meet your expectations.

If you include images in your eBook the book will automatically become longer. It isn't unusual to write a hundred pages (for example), add images and then find your book has gained fifty pages or more!

Remember that you are publishing this as an eBook so the cost of publishing won't increase with every additional page you add. That happens with print on demand publishing for print books, not eBooks. If you have an eBook with many pages and you want to do print on demand, you can print an abridged version to reduce the number of pages printed, or include a CD in the book with "bonus chapters", or send your print buyers to your auto responder to download several chapters.

Images or no images?

If you have bought eBooks, you will have come across some which are filled with only text and others with many images.

You should be aware of one thing—there is no right or wrong way when it comes to images. Quite often it will be determined by the subject. For example, if you are writing an eBook which tells you how to join a particular website as part of the process included in the eBook, it might look a little strange if you don't include screenshots of that website.

Another type of image you see in some eBooks is known as 'filler.' This is an image with no real purpose except to break up the text. You could remove these images and the eBook wouldn't suffer, although they do have their place because they make the text easier on the eye by dividing it up into chunks.

If you plan to use images for filler you consider copyright and royalty free images. Don't assume that pictures on a clip art CD or similar software items are free just because it says so on the cover;

quite often they are only for your personal use. This means you cannot use them for commercial purposes, i.e. anything you intend to make a profit from.

There are websites which provide royalty free photos—but always read the terms and conditions thoroughly before you use them. You will find a good source of royalty free photos in the resources section, but a quick internet search on will reveal others that may be equally useful.

We have seen that the topic of your eBook may dictate if you need images or not. If you are telling people how to build a table, you will want to show them as well, so images would be necessary.

If you decide to add images it is important to maintain balance in the finished product.

What do I mean by balance? Let's say you are reading a book on making money online, and there are three sections. In the first section there are plenty of screenshots and images to show you what the author is talking about.

Once you have read that section, you move on to section two, and there are no images—just pages and pages of text. That text may well be broken down into various sub-sections and paragraphs, but it is almost as if it belongs to a completely different eBook! Where have all the images gone?

Slightly puzzled you move on to the third and final section—and low and behold there are dozens of images again. What's the deal?

I'm sure you can see that while there is nothing intrinsically wrong with doing this, it does lead to an unbalanced eBook. With lots of screenshots in the first section, you expected more in the next section.

This takes your attention away from what you are reading, but if you were reading a balanced book with images in every section, your concentration would be on what the author was telling you—and not on what the author didn't include.

I'm not saying that you should be strict and have one image on every third page as long as you can look through the finished eBook and find that your eye isn't drawn to a huge break between images, or too many images in a short space. You should have an eye-pleasing layout that allows for a smooth read.

And remember if you can spot something irritating, your readers will spot it too.

How is it going to look?

We spoke about the need to have a professional looking cover back in Chapter One, but let's look into more depth now.

Two things are obvious when creating a professional eBook cover, and even if you are going to get a professional graphic designer to create a cover for you—which is highly advised for the best results— you need to provide them with an idea of what you want the eBook cover to look like. The graphic designer may be able to advise you as well, but they likely won't understand your business or your topic.

The two most important things to include on your eBook cover are:

- The title of the eBook

- Your name as the author

There are two basic types to choose from, and they are called serif and sans serif. Serif fonts have curly ends to the letters and are more often favored by most people, even if they don't know it. That's because they are more readable.

But sans serif fonts, the more basic fonts without the curly bits on them, are better for eBooks because they appear cleaner and much easier to read on a computer screen.

Next, think about how you want your cover to look. Something bright and eye catching usually makes people notice and take a closer look at your offer.

Think about the subject of the book and jot down some ideas for some strong images that you could use on the cover. For example, a good image (although it has been used many times before, I'm sure) for an eBook that covers how to make money online would be a stack of money, or several stacks of them all piled up together. Better yet, how about a fistful of dollars—literally!

You want a strong image that evokes emotions in people considering purchasing your eBook, because it will help to speed along the buying process itself.

If you have ideas about the layout and graphics scribble them down and show your graphic designer. The designer will offer suggestions based on your input and will likely create a few drafts of different styles for you to choice from. Remember that this is your eBook, and you have the final say on what goes on the cover.

Next you need to start thinking about how the interior text will look. Remember what I said earlier about putting a border around the edges of each page of your eBook? You will be amazed at the difference this makes to the finished result.

A word of advice—I strongly advise you to make a couple of copies of your eBook every couple of days and store at least one copy on a disk or external drive. It is very easy lose or corrupt large files, so prevent disaster by keeping extra copies.

It is the time to experiment with different fonts to see the differences. Some fonts make your eBook professionally and easy on the eyes.

Make headings and sub-headings stand out using bold and larger font. Using boldface and larger fonts creates distinction between areas, and you can do the same for captions on images as well. Not all images will need a caption, but those that do should have smaller font than the text body font. A smaller font will ensure that no one starts reading the caption thinking they are reading the actual text.

As you can see, there is more to think about than you might have realized. So don't be tempted to publish your eBook until you have figured out how it can look its best.

Think about ways to make certain things stand out as well. Bold and italic font can work well if used in moderation, although you need to be careful because italics don't always look good or readable with certain fonts. The same applies to the size of font that you use as well.

When it comes to the eBook interior (and this goes for any book, not just one that appears in electronic format), some authors feel that almost every square inch of the page needs to be covered in text. It's almost as if the author is worried about having any white space there at all. This is crazy since the cost to publish electronically is the same whether your eBook is 10 pages or 500 hundred.

Some authors try to make a small eBook look bigger by spreading the contents out and using huge font and double spacing each line of text. This creates too much white space and it is obvious to the reader what the author had in mind. However, if you use a decent size font that is easy to read with a reasonable space between lines of text the document will actually be easier on your readers' eyes.

If you aren't sure how to approach this part of the project, take a sample page from your eBook and lay it out in several different ways. Then email it to a few friends and ask them which layout they prefer. It doesn't matter whether they like the actual content or not—after all it could be on a subject they have no particular interest in at all.

Something at the bottom of every page

The footer section of your eBook is a perfect opportunity to communicate with your customers. The best strategy is to include a link to a similar product that the reader may click on and purchase.

The link can point to one of your other products, or to another publisher's product using your affiliate link. This is an excellent marketing opportunity since you have a targeted market seeing your link on every single page of your eBook. If your eBook exceeds the expectations of the reader you will earn their respect and they are more likely to purchase your other products or trust your advice.

You can also include a few words of sales copy to help entice readers to click on the link. For example, if you have a second eBook that you sell on the topic of generating free traffic to your website you could create a link with the text "free traffic secrets the gurus are hiding from you." The entire text would be a link to your sales page.

Conclusion

I'm betting that your head is probably spinning by now, wondering how on earth you are going to publish a bestselling eBook when you have so much to think about before the writing starts. How on earth do people get their books published online so quickly when there is so much to do beforehand?

Systems- once you do this a time or two you will get a system down so that you can pump out eBooks very quickly. At this stage you should concentrate on writing, and keep in mind that the eBook and mini-site must look very professional prior launch.

If you have ideas about what type of images to use while you are writing you should make a note before you forget (and you will forget). If you are using Microsoft Word, you should use the Review tool to track your changes and add comments (like notes to yourself).

For example, if you are writing a section and you think you may add a picture on a certain subject at the end, add a comment to remind you later.

We've covered plenty of ground here, and now you know how to get ready to start writing, which is exactly what we will be doing next.

Chapter 4:
Let's Start Writing!

Yes, it's time to get to the main event—and that's the writing itself. Before we do so, let me make one thing absolutely clear. Don't worry too much if your spelling and grammar aren't perfect. Make good use of the spell checker and grammar checker on your computer, but don't get hung up over every word. I have read plenty of eBooks in the past that have delivered outstanding and extremely revealing and knowledgeable content in less than perfect English. I doubt it harmed their sales much either.

I'm not saying that you shouldn't do your absolute best to make sure everything comes out perfect, but you should remember that the vast majority of people online are looking for information, and they will pay money to the person who can provide them with the answers they are looking for. It's the content that comes first, not the fact that you habitually spell a couple of words wrong.

If you don't feel confident about writing, you can visit one of the many freelance websites that let you post your project and invite people to bid on it. It is then up to you to choose the writer you think would be good for the job, whose bid you are willing to accept and pay.

This is a perfectly legitimate way of writing, known as ghostwriting, and it goes on a lot more often than you might think. For some people, there is nothing more satisfying than writing their own eBook and publishing it to the world. Others would love to have their name on an eBook, but for whom the whole process is too much to cope with. If you consider hiring a ghostwriter and want it published quickly there is no doubt that a professional eBook writer can often accomplish the writing much faster than a novice writer, and usually to a higher standard as well.

Assuming you will do the writing yourself, let's take a look at how you can really connect with your readers and develop an eBook to be proud of.

Optimize Microsoft Word with these tips

Working with Microsoft Word can be a blessing and a curse as we all know. There are ways to reduce the hair pulling that are quite simple, and your heart will appreciate the lower blood pressure.

- Turn off "Automatically create drawing canvas when inserting Auto Shapes" (Tools>Options>General tab>uncheck box)

- Adjust macro virus protection to medium or higher (Tools>Options>Security>Macro Security)

- Turn off "Allow Fast Saves" and "Allow Background Saves" (Tools>Options>Save>uncheck boxes)

- Turn on "Save Auto Recover Info" (Tools>Options>Save>check box and adjust to every 5 minutes)

- Turn off "Keep Track of Formatting" (Tools>Options>Edit>uncheck box)

- Turn on "Use Smart Cut and Paste" (Tools>Options>Edit>check box)

- Turn off "When Selecting, Automatically Select Entire Word" (Tools>Options>Edit>uncheck box)

- Turn off "Use Smart Paragraph Selection" (Tools>Options>Edit>uncheck box)

- Turn off "Check Spelling As You Type" and "Check Grammar As You Type" (Tools>Options>Spelling & Grammar>uncheck box). Just remember to manually run the spelling and grammar tool after completing your draft copy

- Turn off "Wrap to Window" and "Draft Font" (Tools>Options>View>uncheck boxes)

- Turn off "Draft Output" (Tools>Options>Print>uncheck box)

The above modifications greatly increase the stability of Microsoft Word documents, which will make your life much easier especially if you are going to become a prolific writer.

Set the page size for print on demand

If you plan to publish your book in print using print on demand services you must set the layout in Word. The most common book paperback book trim, or size, is 6 x 9 inches in the US. To set the page size in Word: File>Page Setup>Layout>adjust the width and height.

Tips for properly formatting text

The rules for formatting vary between print and online viewing for obvious reasons. Following these simple tips will help you project an image of a professional writer.

- Quotes and apostrophes should be curly when in print form. Many writers are fine with straight quotes in electronic form since Word can be buggy with the quotes. This is a bit of a hot topic with some writers and web designers, but the short story is that curly quotes and apostrophes are correct. The straight, or "dumb", quotes were created with the invention of the typewriter. The typewriter didn't have room for the curly quotes, and it certainly didn't have room for an extra key for the left curly quote. Some of the less effective HTML converters will garble your curly quotes and they will tell you to use straight quotes, such as www.articlemarketer.com. This is due to their inability to convert the curly quote, not because it is correct. Tools>Auto Correct Options>Auto Format>check.

- If you are using Auto Format you need to watch for curls that go the wrong way, especially in cases such as '08 for 2008.

- To insert proper trademark, registered, and copyright symbols just do the key combination Control-Alt-T/R/C.

- Prime and double prime (angled straight quotes and apostrophes) are used for foot and inch and minutes and seconds. An option is to italicize straight quotes.

- Underlining is rarely used in print.

- Don't use more than one space after a sentence.

- Paragraphs in print should be indented ¼ or slightly more, but less than ½ and inch, with no extra space between paragraphs. For electronic books block paragraphs are common with no indent and a space between paragraphs equal to 1.5 - 2 times the height between sentences. If you use line spacing of 1.5 rather than the default 1.0, you will need a larger space between paragraphs.

- Adjust paragraph spacing using Format>Paragraph>Spacing and adjust the before and after. You can also adjust the line spacing on this page.

- Justify your text for a neat clean look in print and digital.

- Fonts for eBooks should be sans serif, which is easier to read in electronic form. Popular choices are Aerial, Verdana, Tahoma, Courier, and Helvetica. Verdana was designed specifically for clarity and easy reading on a computer.

- Fonts for print books should be serif. Popular choices are Times Roman Numeral, Georgia, Century Schoolbook, Sabon, Garamond, and Palatino. You can differentiate headings using sans serif font for headings in print and serif font for headings in digital format.

- Font size for eBooks should be between 11 and 13 points. If you are reading this book electronically you are reading Verdana 12 point font for the body text. If you are holding this book in your hand, you are reading Georgia 12 point font. Keep in mind that different fonts are different sizes even at the same point size. For example, Times Roman Numeral 12 point is much smaller than Georgia 12 point.

- Line spacing is the amount of space between sentences in a paragraph. The default in Word is 1.0 and the shortcut in the reviewing toolbar offers quick pick options in increments of 0.5, so that is 1.0, 1.5, 2.0, etc. You can also fine tune the setting in Format>Paragraph>line spacing where you can type in increments of 0.1 and make certain that you choose "Exactly" from the drop down menu. Typically for eBooks line spacing of 1.2 - 1.5 provides enough whitespace to make reading the text easier.

I am currently reviewing the first draft of this book, and I realized that I forgot to add, and do, a great trick with Word. Word does not handle justification well. Word will only stretch, not shrink, the space between words, not letters. This weakness can create extra large spaces between words, but you can fix this by going to Tools>Options>Compatibility>check "do full justification like Word-Perfect 6.x for Windows". Prior to checking that box my page count was 286, after checking the box 278, so it tightened up the text considerably.

You should also include a border for each page in your eBooks, except for the title page. I can't stand the bright and thick borders that some authors seem to love. They seem unprofessional to me, maybe I am crazy. I like a simple thin sold black 28.

(Format>Borders and Shading>Borders Tab>chose box, black, and 1 point width.

For more information on preparing your file for print I recommend Aaron Sheperd's "Perfect Pages" book.

Focus on one section at a time

Remember the structure we were discussing in the previous chapter? Well, once you have come up with a structure for your own eBook, it's time to take it out and use it to start piecing together the sections of your eBook as you write it.

You'll probably have a structure that is written on a single sheet of 8 ½" x 11" paper, but don't focus on the entire structure when it is time to sit down and start writing. The key here is to look at the very first chunk of that structure and focus on that only.

Why? It's because you will get through the writing process far more easily if you do. For example, you concentrate on the entire eBook, even though you have just started to write the introduction. Quickly you will start thinking about later chapters and sections that will affect your focus on the current section that you are writing.

And that means a greater chance of making mistakes, missing out information you wanted to include, and so on. In short, trying to focus on the whole outline is the quickest and easiest ways to totally confuse you.

If you can't stop yourself from doing this, print out of the first section of the eBook that you are writing. Nothing else—just that first bit. Then read through it a few times and get your head around what you need to write about. Scribble down a few notes and ideas as they come to you—it will make the process easier, and it's a sure sign that your brain is starting to focus on just this one section of your eBook.

Even if you have worries about writing a particular section later on, don't think about it until you get to that section.

It gets a lot easier with practice. You will find that you develop tunnel vision where you will be completely absorbed with the section of the eBook you are working on.

You'll soon find out more about the editing process as well, but I want to say that you should be aware that there will be an editing process. Some people don't allow for editing, and they think they can just sit down and write a book without going back through it to make sure everything is just right.

Even if your writing style flows beautifully and you can get things pretty much spot on at the first attempt (which very few people can actually do in practice), you can be sure that it is virtually impossible to write something perfectly the first time around without making some mistakes.

It may be typing mistakes—very easy to do even with a spell checker, which doesn't always get the meaning you want to imbue in your words exactly right—or it may be a simple factual error. The point is that when you are in the heat of writing and the words are flowing from your fingertips and onto the keyboard, you may well make a few errors that you won't pick up until later on. And if you aren't going to go back and do any editing, then it will be your readers who will spot those errors and point them out to you.

This could happen anyway since it is not always easy to be absolutely 100% correct throughout the whole eBook, but you should do your best to make your writing the best that you can make it before you release the eBook. So stay tuned for that editing section and make sure you don't skip it.

You might think it's a good idea to edit one section at a time as you are focused on it, but in fact this isn't usually a good idea. You are better off working through each section at a time and get the whole eBook written first—then you can start polishing it.

More benefits to writing in different chunks

There's another benefit? You bet there is!

I've mentioned that writing a whole eBook can be a daunting task, and I have included a chapter full of techniques and advice that will help you make sure you get to the end of your own personal journey. That's coming up next.

But you see, if you are intending to write an eBook that is, say, a hundred or so pages in length, you might have trouble thinking about how you can fit that into your schedule. Let's be honest, the chances are that you will either have a full-time job right now, or a part-time job and other commitments, or you are a full-time house person looking after your family. Whatever situation you are in, you probably won't automatically have several hours a day that you can fit your writing into.

If you have a huge eBook that you want to write, you will probably be wondering whether you could ever do it given your current commitments. But if you have a number of chunks that need to be written—each one of which may only be five to ten pages at most—well, that's a lot more manageable, wouldn't you say?

In fact, you could probably look at your schedule and figure out that one five page chunk could even be written this week, if you snagged a few minutes here and there to get it done.

See how this works? It's all about giving yourself an easier journey, and you'll see more about how to do that in the next chapter.

Writing for an audience of one

While many book publishers might want a more efficient and practical writing style, you don't need to worry about that when you are writing eBooks to sell directly to the general public. In fact, the friendlier you can be the better.

While it will hopefully be the case that you will be selling thousands of copies of your eBook to people all over the world, you don't want to be thinking about that when you sit down to write it. That thought can stop you in your tracks more surely than anything else! I mean you could literally have people in all kinds of different countries buying and downloading your eBook to read, so how on earth do you manage to appeal to all of them?

Here's what you do.

Think about the topic of your eBook for a moment. Let's say you've decided to write about saving money on your groceries. Now I want you to imagine that someone (one person) is sitting right next to you, and they want to know everything you know about saving money in this way.

What would you do if they were actually in the room? You'd start talking to them, right? Of course you would. You'd start chatting away about various aspects of saving money on groceries, including some tips and tricks you've discovered yourself about the best times to go shopping, making the most of bulk deals, and so on.

You'd tell him/her all you know, and it would be very conversational, purely because you would be talking to him/her only—and that is how you need to write your eBook. You need to write for an audience of one. If you write this way, you'll end up with a nice relaxed and friendly style of writing that will really appeal to people. It's easy to read, and it tells them everything they want to know.

When you sit down to write, focus your attention on the one person who wants to know everything about your subject. Writing this way can take a while to get used to, but it takes your attention away from the horrifying thought that there may actually be thousands of people out there somewhere waiting to read your eBook. If you aim it at all of them, you won't please anyone—and yet if you aim it at one single person, he/she will understand your message and be drawn into it more firmly.

Call it the lowest common denominator. People who purchase your eBook are looking for the same information. So focus on one generic person and imagine he/she is sitting right there with you whenever you sit down to write.

That's the first step to great writing. Now let's continue to the next step.

Keeping positive

Have you ever read a book of any kind that was all doom and gloom and scare tactics? Depressing, isn't it?

You don't want to depress your reader; I'm pretty sure you'll end up writing other eBooks in the future, and it would be nice to think that you could sell more eBooks to that same reader. You won't be able to do that if all they remember is how low they felt once they'd finished reading your first one!

So we need to stay upbeat, fresh and positive right throughout the whole writing process, from the first page to the last. Don't forget that your eBook must solve some kind of problem for the reader, and whether that is getting rid of money worries, growing better tomatoes or getting rid of spots, you need to stay positive, otherwise they will begin to wonder if you can solve their problem.

You also need to be sure you don't overdo it though. I've read eBooks where the tone has been so positive that every other sentence has ended in an exclamation mark, and the writer has obviously got so overexcited he/she can't control himself/herself!!!!

The secret is to be upbeat and positive without overdoing it, and it's not as hard as you might think. Save the "wow" stuff for your sales letter and keep your eBook solid and encouraging, and you won't go wrong.

If you focus on the negatives, it will start to affect you as well, and your writing will lose its strength and energy. But if you concentrate on all the great things you have to tell people—just think of that method you've got for saving 50% off your current grocery bill for example—that positively will shine through your writing and captivate people as surely as any traditional bestseller will.

You're helping a lot of people by writing your eBook, make no mistake about it. You can really change some lives here, no matter what you have chosen to write about.

Writing with emotion and passion

This should be easy if you have picked a topic that you love and you know a lot about. People can usually tell when you love what you are writing about because it shines through your writing in ways that are hard to pin down. You can tell when that passion is there, and you can tell when it's not, but you'll never quite be able to put your finger on exactly what it is that makes it sound that way.

While you may eventually write eBooks about subjects you don't know much about and have to research, if you start with subjects you do possess a lot of knowledge about, you will find it easier to get yourself motivated and enthusiastic when you write. Over time your writing style will develop, and you'll find the words will come more easily.

The main thing to remember is to keep that enthusiasm pumping through your writing. You can transfer that feeling to anyone else through your writing if it is genuine within yourself, so work on spreading the knowledge you are acquiring.

I am going to reiterate here that you shouldn't worry too much about how your writing comes out initially. Just let it flow and pour out onto the page—you can go back and read it later to check that it makes sense and that there are no errors. If you try to edit it as you go along, you'll lose that flow, and your enthusiasm may to drop off. Then you run the risk of your writing becoming flat as a result.

Just remember that you have an amazing opportunity to share knowledge with people you have never met, that could actually change their lives. Isn't that amazing? Keep that in mind, and you'll have no trouble being enthusiastic about your writing sessions!

Making sure you stay on track

I'm not talking about when or where you are writing here or how often, I'm talking about the subject itself.

When you sit down to start writing your eBook, you will find that it's easy to get started writing about your subject. It might not be the most polished piece of writing ever, and it might be a long way from being perfect (at least at this stage), but it will be on topic, and it will be a good start.

Believe me when I say it is very easy to drift off from your subject. Make sure you are always writing about a related aspect of your topic. If it doesn't belong in your eBook, then out it goes—no matter how good that particular paragraph or sentence might be.

It is one thing to be relaxed and comfortable in your writing, but it is quite another to start waffling about something that has no place being in your eBook at all. So stick to this rule and look closely at your work when editing to make sure you didn't go down the wrong path.

Getting into more detail

We've covered many pointers to keep in mind during the writing process, now let's find out how you should approach various sections and parts of your eBook.

I recommend reading through this entire section and once you actually start writing, come back to this part to double check the tips and advice to help you with the section you are writing.

Title Page

The title page is page number one of your eBook, but it doesn't have a page number listed on it. The title page also does not have a footer like the rest of the pages. To prevent the page number and footer from appearing on the title page in Word, while the cursor is on the title page, go to file, page setup, click different first page. Please note: Odd numbers pages are always on the right side of the eBook. This is very important to look professional and especially if you plan to create a physical book using print on demand (POD). Formatting for the title page can vary, but once you choose a format you should stick to it. If you want to make it fast and simple, you can follow my format.

I use Verdana 24 point starting at the eighth line from the top of page. No bold and no underline, centered on page, and only a single space between title and subtitle. Near the bottom in Verdana font in14 point, I include the author's name; next line is publishing company; and next line is state/province and country, or city and state/province, each centered on the page. Insert a page break after this last text by clicking Insert>Break>Page Break so that the copyright page will start on page two.

Copyright Page

In physical books the copyright page is always located on a left page immediately following the title page. Since you need to include some copyright information in your eBook I suggest setting it up as you would for a physical book. If you decide to sell physical books in the future your copyright page will be set up properly. I used the sans serif font Tahoma at 12 point to change it up for this page. Include the word copyright, year, and your first and last name to meet copyright protection requirements. To create the symbol ©, hold down the control, alt, and C keys. So, that would be "Copyright © 2009 by Your Name". You don't need to file your work to have it protected by copyright. Your work is automatically protected by copyright laws. Add your International Standard Book Number (ISBN) if you have one. You may also include trademark information, acknowledgements, graphic credits, legal notices, disclaimer, and a link to a blog or website where readers can receive updates. Add a page break at the bottom of this page. The copyright page will have the page number two on the bottom, and it should also include your eBook's footer.

Automatically create Table of Contents

If you use the header styles H1, H2, H3 for chapter and section titles, you can automatically insert a professional looking table of contents. Add Table of Contents to top of page, centered. Then click on Insert>Reference>Index and Tables>Table of Contents tab. Here you can choose from several formats and options. Don't forget to update the table of contents after editing your eBook by right clicking on table of contents page and selecting Update Field>Update Entire Field.

Automatically create Index

If you plan to sell the book in print, you will definitely want to create an index. Go to the page where you want to insert the index and Insert>Reference>Index and Tables>choose your format, which is typically 2 columns for print books.

Introduction

An eBook introduction may be less than a page long, or they may be several pages long, but they all serve to introduce the reader to the eBook as a whole.

They don't include any of the information that will be found in future chapters; rather, they will touch on some of the things that will be found in the main part of the eBook.

The introduction basically serves to generate interest for the rest of the eBook, and it usually informs the reader about what they can hope to achieve by the time they have finished reading the eBook.

There is another advantage of the introduction as well. You can offer the introduction as a free download from your eBook mini-site to generate interest from potential buyers. This works well when people come across your mini-site, and they are considering whether or not to buy your eBook, the offer of reading the first chapter for free might just persuade them to purchase the eBook! You can also require the submission of an email address to gain access to the free introduction chapter, which can be used for email marketing later on.

If you use your introduction as a marketing tool it needs to do your eBook justice to convince readers to purchase the full eBook. You shouldn't promise anything that you can't deliver on, or tell the readers that something is coming up and then not include it in the eBook. But if you can tell them your eBook will make a difference to their live, then they will be going straight to the real meat of the eBook once they have finished reading the introduction itself.

Chapter Headings

Every eBook should have a Table of Contents. The headings for each chapter or section of the eBook will appear here, so it is important to make sure they are enticing and attractive to the eye so that the reader is drawn in from the first page.

Chapter headings don't need to be clever or flashy—in fact it often works better if they aren't—but they should tell people exactly what they can expect from each section even before they get there.

As you see with this book, the chapter headings are quite straightforward and simple—and yet they tell you exactly what you will discover in that chapter. Another benefit of having good solid headings is easy of navigating through the eBook by clicking on the links in the Table of Contents to find information he/she want to read again.

Writing style

It might take you a while to discover your writing style if you haven't written an eBook before. If you aren't a writer, you will probably try unconsciously to emulate the writing styles of writers that you admire, and somewhere along the way you will develop your own style without even realizing.

Should you worry about your writing style when you set out to start writing?

No. I don't think this is the most important part of writing any kind of book; the most important part is to give readers a good experience and make sure you give them the knowledge that will enable them to improve their lives.

If you force your writing style, it usually ends up as a disaster, so you are much better off concentrating your energies on gathering all the information you need, and not coping anyone's style. It will come to you eventually, and when it does you will know it. You'll have a distinct way of writing about things that no one else will have, and if people like that style, they will be more likely to buy more eBooks from you in the future.

Focus on a practical style to begin with. Make sure you tell people what you want them to know in simple enough terms. Think about what most people are likely to know and don't talk down to them by explaining something that doesn't need to be explained.

For example, everyone knows that if you go crazy making purchases with your credit card, you will eventually hit your limit and the card will be rejected. So don't tell them this as a statement. If you really need to include obvious information, try doing so as an offhand remark, much like I have done above. I have stated the obvious in that first sentence, but by prefacing it with those two words, 'everyone knows', I have taken out any condescending tone that might have been interpreted otherwise.

Using examples

Examples can really spice up an eBook. Most topics can use examples to connect more effectively with your readers.

Examples can also help your readers' understanding of the information you are trying to convey by phrasing things in a different manner. The instance with the credit card and going over the limit that I used to demonstrate how you could give information to the reader without talking down to them. By using a good example like this one, I can be sure that the reader will understand the information.

If I was to explain something complex without giving examples, then there would be no way of knowing whether or not the reader really understood. That's why examples are so important—they keep your reader on track and make the whole subject much easier to understand.

The number of examples you need will depend on how complex your subject is. There is no hard and fast rule on how many or few you should include; some chapters may need several while others might require none at all. Rely on your judgment—and you can always ask for some advice from someone you trust as to whether or not you have the balance right.

Conclusions

A conclusion has the role of wrapping up the eBook and making sure that all the points you wanted to mention have been included. It closes the eBook nicely rather than ending abruptly.

As with the introduction, there is no set number of pages that the conclusion should have, other than it will generally be shorter than any chapter or section within the main part of the eBook.

If you have written an eBook offering advice on how readers can do something better, or achieve something, or better their lives in some way, then you should certainly use the conclusion of the eBook as an opportunity to encourage them to take action. Unfortunately, there are a lot of people who buy eBooks on many different subjects, read them thoroughly and then fail to take any action at all.

Give readers something to think about as they reach the end of your eBook. Urge them to take action today to make their lives better. Tell them how you took your first steps to getting a better life (which should of course be relevant to the subject of your eBook). Give readers a final push before you leave them to forge ahead on their own.

So there you have it—a concise guide to getting started and writing your eBook. Once you have the plan laid out, and you know how to tackle each and every section, you will be creating pages of content quickly. In the next chapter I will reveal how to make sure you finish your eBook!

Chapter 5:
Getting from Start to Finish

It's been a great journey so far hasn't it? You might already have started writing if you have stopped reading this book for long enough to get ideas together, research it as far as is necessary and completed your plan.

I am going to make the whole process much easier for you by sharing some tips and techniques I have built up over the years. These have been gathered through writing many different materials—from articles, eBooks, and physical book.

These tips will help you to get from the beginning of your eBook to the end. Let's get started and see how we can make this journey an easier one to navigate.

Getting from start to finish can be the hardest

You'll remember I spoke about procrastination earlier. Procrastination is a nasty little beast that needs to be slain if you are going to complete an eBook.

We are going to tackle this problem, so that you will know what to do to get past them.

Techniques for staying the course

I recommend that you read through this section of the book thoroughly, word for word.

There is a lot to digest here, and I have tried to include as many solutions as I can—many of which I have encountered and solved myself during my own writing career.

So are you ready? Then let's get started.

"What if I get stuck on a particular section?"

An easy solution is to persevere with writing the section you are having difficulty with. It is difficult to carry on without stopping for at least a short period of time, and sometimes a short break is necessary to give you time to gather your thoughts and decide how to move forward.

If you find yourself staring at your computer screen for more than five minutes and you haven't made any progress, that could be a sign that you need to stop and move on to another section.

That doesn't mean you stop writing your eBook. If you still have time to write that day, all you need to do is glance at the structure you have created for your eBook and move on to another section.

While fiction writers have little choice in having to move from one chapter onto the next in order, non-fiction writers have more flexibility. You know exactly what will go in each section—thanks to that structure you carefully created—so there is no reason why you cannot move on to another part of the eBook where you can build momentum.

This method will get the eBook written faster, and you can still go back and edit it all later to make certain the eBook flows well. When you go back to the section you abandoned you will likely find it easier to write.

"What if I can't write anything at all?"

If you have writer's block you should take a break. Finish writing early for the day if you need to, but don't be tempted to skip a day.

Avoid writing when you have writer's block. Trying to fight through this can make the problem worse and can cause the problem to continue for much longer. Try again during your next scheduled writing session. Most instances of writer's block don't last long.

If you continue to have writer's block try reading about your subject instead of writing for the day. This can renew your enthusiasm that you had when you started writing the eBook.

The issue could also be caused by something else going on in your life that is drawing your attention away from your writing. It's possible to feel guilty about spending time writing if you have other things on your mind that require your attention. In this situation try to focus on solving the issue before starting your day's writing session.

"How do I get the eBook construction right?"

When writing flows well it is easy to read and pulls you from the beginning through to the end—almost without the reader realizing it. This is a goal you need to have as a writer, because it will make your eBook easier and more enjoyable to read.

You'll likely find yourself wondering whether that sentence on page 3 had too many words in it. And what about that paragraph on page 6? Was it too long? Was a piece in section two so long that it will probably bore everyone who reads it?

The one thing you need to remember is that it doesn't matter how many words are in each sentence you write, or how many sentences you have in each paragraph. Your objective is to get your eBook written, even if that means having a fifty two word sentence in chapter one and a paragraph that is three pages long in chapter four.

Just get it all down on paper and let the editing process take care of these questions. That is all you need to think about. Just keep reminding yourself that you are getting the information down first; there will be plenty of time to work on form and polishing it later on.

"What if I have a fear of writing?"

This isn't writer's block. Writer's block happens when you sit down to write and nothing happens. A fear of writing is when you will do anything to stop yourself from starting to write in the first place.

Here are some common fears that stop people from writing:

- What if it's not good enough?
- What if I get it wrong?

- What if someone else has already written this and I haven't discovered it?

- What if I don't know enough to write about this subject?

There more reasons, but these show you how a fear of writing can stop your eBook from ever seeing the light of day.

To overcome your fear force yourself to write a single paragraph of three or four lines. That's it. Don't worry about how much you may have wanted to write that day: just write one small paragraph, after which you will get up from your desk and go and do something else.

A paragraph is so small that it might only take you a few seconds, a minute, or perhaps five minutes. By the time you have finished that paragraph you will probably have forgotten about your initial fear of writing anyway, because the power of what you are writing will have pulled you in and you will be on to the next paragraph... and the one after that too.

The trick is to find a way to get going, even if that only requires the smallest effort initially. Once you have done that you will be off and away.

Same time tomorrow...

This technique helps to prevent writer's block and fear of writing, so if you use it you will find the writing process easier and more enjoyable.

Many professional writers write at the same time every day. Some get up early to write, while others work into the early hours of the morning. But no matter when they start, many of them will start at the exact same time every day. This practice creates a habit you will soon get used to, and it makes your writing more productive.

Not everyone reading this book will be able to choose the time they write in the same way as many other full-time writers can. If you have a full-time job, then you will have to fit your writing in around that. But it is important to try and schedule a writing session at the same time each day if possible.

Here are some ideas you could try:

- Get up half an hour earlier each morning.
- Take half an hour in your lunch time to write.
- Start writing for a short time as soon as you get home from work.
- If you take the train or bus, why not scribble down some ideas or write a few paragraphs on the journey.
- Stay up half an hour later each night to write once everyone else has gone to sleep.
- Miss one of those TV programs you're hooked on!

Rather than thinking that this process is a drag on your lifestyle just keep in mind the benefits you will experience once you start selling your eBooks.

Don't leave long gaps in between writing sessions

Writing a small amount every day is the best solution to getting your eBook finished quickly and keeping the dreaded writer's block at arm's length, it isn't always possible to fit writing into your schedule like this.

If you decide to have weekends off, make sure you write every day during the week. The worst thing you can do is to have a prolonged gap in between writing sessions, because it is harder to get started again.

I'm sure you know the feeling you get when you have been on holiday for a week or two, and you have to go back to work. That first day is quite difficult to get through.

The exact same thing happens with your writing, and because it is up to you to get yourself in front of your computer and put words on the screen, you will find that it is all too easy to let it slide for another day before you get started.

And it can be a slippery slope too.

So make sure you write as often as you can—it's probably better to write for fifteen minutes every single day than it is to write for an hour three days a week, because that regular effort will keep the book and your writing fresh in your mind.

Are you writing too much...?

It can happen! Sometimes you will be flying on a particular passage and although you have already completed your required time or number of pages for the day, it makes sense to carry on can while the words are flowing.

But if that results in you sitting in front of your computer screen for hours trying to force the words out, it won't help you at all. If you find yourself in this situation, make sure you take a break every now and then so you can recharge your mental batteries.

The best thing to do is to go out and get a breath of fresh air. Even if all you do is go and put the kettle on for a hot drink and wander out into the garden while you're waiting for it to boil, you would be amazed at how much clearer your head will feel as a result.

Take some deep breaths of fresh air, and really make the most of it. Go post office, take the dog for a walk, or jog round the block for a lap or two.

Stop trying to write... and talk instead

Still stuck on how to write a particular section? Another technique you can try, but you might want to wait until you are alone!

The trick – rather than writing down what you want to say, you try saying it out loud instead. This might sound crazy, but it can really help you break through a block.

When you think about it, what do you do when you can't think of what you want to type? Answer – you don't type anything.

Okay, so what do you do when you can't think of what you want to say out loud? Answer – you normally talk around the subject, coming up with lots of umms and aahs while you try to find a way to get the words out.

Imagine there is someone sitting opposite you that you need to explain your point to. They are waiting for you to say something, and the last thing you want to do (it's really in our human nature) is to sit there in silence. So you start to mention certain words that might help you. You try to start putting into words what you are feeling and what it is you want to say.

You will feel silly in the beginning, but it won't last long once you start to get the answers you need. Just make sure you are sitting in front of your computer so that when the words start to flow you can start typing them.

Focus on the benefits of a finished eBook

Writers concentrate on the task at hand—writing this chapter, finishing that sentence, and so on. The big goal at the end of all these tasks is to publish an eBook and generate revenue.

Imagine what that will be like. In fact, think about the amount of money you would like to earn from the sale of your eBook, even if that amount is a large one, and you're not sure you will actually reach it. Many people have gone from writing their first eBook to creating a whole series that sell extremely well.

If you aren't comfortable with dreaming big, think about the price you will put on each eBook and work from there. So let's say for example you are going to sell your eBook for $39, and let's suppose you make just 100 sales. That isn't very many at all, and you can certainly imagine selling 100 copies I'm sure.

That works out to $3,900. Suddenly those 100 sales have brought in a significant amount of money. What would you do with that cash?

Think about what you would spend it on and jot down as many ideas as you can think of. This is a great exercise to get into, and it is extremely motivating!

Here are some ideas to get you started:

- Buying a gadget or toy you have always wanted.

- Taking a trip with the family.

- Paying a chunk off a credit card.

- Paying a down payment on a new vehicle.

- Funding the kids' college fund.

- Reinvesting in your internet marketing business.

Once you have something in mind, find a picture of it. Find a photo of a small stack of money online and stick a picture of a credit card next to it, for example. Place the pictures next to your computer, or wherever you write, to serve as a reminder of what you will be able to do once those first ten sales come in.

To watch others become successful check out www.warriorforum.com/warrior—special—offers—forum where many good products are offered at a discounted price and can haul in many thousands in a couple of days. Now that is motivation.

Do you see how powerful this can be? Once you have found the right motivational trigger you won't be able to stop writing!

But your end result here refers to what you might want to achieve as an eBook writer in the future. Do you want to stop once you have written your first eBook? I doubt it!

The truth is that you will probably get hooked on writing eBooks and start to explore other subjects to write about and sell to your customers, and anyone else who expresses an interest in your writing.

Don't be afraid to dream about the things you could achieve in the future. You could be starting to build towards a website containing all your eBooks on a single subject—as well as all those mini-sites of course—right now, without even realizing it.

But you can also visualize what the finished eBook will look like. Imagine seeing it and reading it on your own computer screen. Just think about that dynamic and sales pulling cover that really tells people what the book is all about and makes it irresistible to buy.

This exercise keeps your motivation burning to the end of your eBook and it will give you useful ideas on how to present your eBook and give it a cover that will do it justice.

Once you have done your visualizing, make sure you jot down any great ideas you had that really would look good on the finished product!

And if all else fails...

You can think of ideas for your next eBooks while you are writing the current one. You may as well do the research for 10 eBooks that are related so that you can cross promote each title. Your next eBook will promote eBook the first one and so on. This is also great because you will already have an email list of potential buyers from eBook buyers.

While this isn't necessary, it is a strong strategy for long term success, and it helps to give you some variety if you are like me and get bored easily.

Another idea is try thinking about how you are going to promote your finished eBook and start jotting down some ideas for how to promote it.

So you see there are plenty of things you can do to keep yourself motoring towards the end of your eBook, and the moment when you can finally put it on sale.

What should you edit as you go along?

I have mentioned editing in passing previously, and the very next chapter will deal with it in full, but it is worth mentioning here that there are a few things you can watch out for, and not to watch out for, while you are writing the first draft of your eBook.

First, there is spelling. Leave spell checker off until you have a complete draft manuscript. If you attempt to spell check as you write, you will lose focus and flow, so don't do it.

If you aren't sure about the accuracy of a piece of information as you write it, insert a comment (Insert>Comment) or highlight the text so that you won't forget to come back later and research the information.

Incidentally, that's a great way to keep track of things you want to do once you start editing. If there is anything you aren't sure of, you can highlight it in a different color and then go back to it later.

That's really all you need to be thinking about at this stage; the main goal here and the most challenging thing of all is to get something down that will serve as your first draft. Once you have done that, you will have something solid that you can work on—even if you think it will take a fair bit of work to get it to look good and to end up with the final result you wanted in the first place.

Once you complete a draft of the entire eBook you will want to start using the Track Changes tool (Tools>Track Changes) before you start editing. This will allow you to clearly see the changes that you are making for all future drafts. When the next draft is complete, just click on the Track Changes tool bar check mark drop down menu and select Accept All Changes in Document. I save each draft as a different copy identified by the date at the end of the file name.

Working out a timetable to complete the work

Unless you happen to have the world's best job and you only work an hour a day for full-time money, I'm willing to bet that your days are already pretty full. I've already touched on how important it is to write regularly. The world is full of people who would write an eBook 'if only they had the time…' and unless you want to become one of them, you need to make sure that you will have the time—no matter what it takes.

Here's what you do.

Get a blank sheet of paper or open up a new Excel file and divide it up into seven sections, one for each day of the week.

This idea might seem a bit basic, but it is the single best way to make sure you do have the time to write. Many people sit down to write their first eBook, and they think they'll have no problem fitting the required amount of writing into their day.

And then reality hits them. They have to take their kids to school each day. They're too tired when they get in from work. And tomorrow always seems to be a better day than today.

Here's what we're going to do to make sure you complete your chores and commitments and still find the time you need to get that first eBook written and out there and making cash for you.

First, divide each day up into hourly segments. Half hourly is even better. Start from the earliest time you get up each day and go up until you normally go to bed.

Then spend some time going through all the chores and responsibilities you have each day. Try to go through each day of the week and think about anything tasks that occur on a weekly and a daily basis. This will help to make sure you don't miss anything. A good example is taking the trash out. If you have to do this each week, it might seem like a minor chore, but we all know it takes longer than you might think to empty all those bins indoors and take everything out!

Start with the obvious commitments and add them to your timetable first. Work will probably be the most obvious one, but if you work from nine until five every day, make sure you block out the time it takes you to get ready before you go, travel to work, travel home again and then get changed when you get in. Once you have added in all that additional time you might find you have to block out from 7am until 7pm.

Once you have written down everything you can think of that you do each day or each week, highlight the free time you have left. Are there any segments of time there (even if they only last for fifteen minutes or so) that are consistent every day of the week?

If there are, then you have a candidate for the ideal writing session, occurring the same time every day, as we read about a couple of pages back. Some people find it best to write Monday to Friday. Other people prefer to write on weekends.

Once you have a timetable organized stick it up next to your computer and try it out for a week to see how it actually works out. Have you picked the best time to write? Do you function better first thing in the morning and therefore writing at 6:15 am is no problem for you? Maybe you thought that writing at 11:00 pm was your best bet... but by the time you get there you are too tired to really think straight.

Don't worry if your first schedule doesn't work out—and don't quit either. Try out something else instead. Everyone has some free time each day.

Chapter 6:
Tips and Techniques for Professional Editing

Wow—you have finally finished your eBook. Well done! You have written every single one of those chunks you jotted down as part of your outline (aren't you glad you took the time to do that now?). Simply by getting to this stage you have achieved more than many who never get beyond the idea stage.

Now it's time to congratulate yourself on a great job and forget all about that eBook.

Hey, don't panic, you're still going to be selling it—you just need to check it over first and make sure it's ready for your readers. If you put it aside for a couple of days, the editing process will be a lot easier, because you'll find that errors you've made (no matter what type they are) will be easier to spot. And you'll find that changing the odd word here and there will lead to a smoother and much more pleasant read.

Giving yourself a break from the whole process will also give you a chance to recharge your batteries for the editing process, so take a break—you earned it!

The importance of editing

Why do we edit eBooks?

It's a simple question, but there are lots of answers. Perhaps the answer that rolls everything into a neat package is this one:

"To make them the best that they can be."

And if that isn't good enough for you then how about this: if you write poorly and your content is of little value to anyone, you won't make it in this business. Your first eBooks can make or break your career in a hurry. If you publish a high quality eBook that is well written and provides valuable and useful information to your niche market, you will build a reputation. Once you have a reputation, your affiliates will promote almost anything that you publish, and more affiliates will sign up to get in on the action.

Even if you are exceptionally good at writing and your first draft is pretty much the same as your final draft, you will still need to edit because you have to pick up on those typos, change words here and there and generally smooth it out a little.

Some people will need to do more editing than others, and you will get to know how good your first draft is once you get more experience. But we are going to look at the whole editing process in this chapter so that you get a good idea of what to expect when you do it yourself.

Editing is very important if you want people to take your work seriously. Amazingly, some people will publish an eBook without bothering to edit it. The author has the money, so why worry?

Understandably you don't tend to see too many of these writers hanging around for very long. This is because the people who buy from them once won't buy from them again—because they want an eBook with a more professional edge. And the affiliates that promote your book will disappear on you in the search of quality products to promote.

Every now and then someone breaks this rule and publishes an eBook that is pretty dreadful in presentation, but they get away with it because the information contained in it is so explosive and so useful to the reader that they are willing to overlook that shortcoming. For example, I once read a book that was very poorly written, and there were a shocking number of simple grammar errors. But I got through the eBook because I found the content interesting, and apparently so did other buyers as the eBook sold very well.

Don't try to get away without editing. Always strive to make your eBooks the best that you can. You will be rewarded if you do this.

How do you know what to edit?

After taking your break from finishing the first draft of your eBook, the first thing you should do is to re-read it from start to finish. When you do, ask yourself the following questions:

- Have you spell checked everything?

- Have you written for one person throughout?

- Have you kept things upbeat and positive?

- Have you included everything that needs to be in there?

- Have you gone off-topic at all?

- Have you repeated yourself where you shouldn't?

These are the main points to consider when you are editing. If you have read what I have revealed so far in this book, you should find that there won't be a huge amount of editing to do. Most people think their eBook will be horrendous... and yet after they have had a couple of days to unwind from the writing process they are usually quite surprised at what they have written!

Watch for certain points though. If you have strayed into an area that really shouldn't be in there (say for example you're writing that eBook on saving money on groceries, and you've inadvertently added in a section on reducing your costs on your cell phone), then take it out—you can always keep it for your next eBook.

If you find the writing less positive in any section, make sure you modify it to be more positive.

This is probably one of the hardest parts of editing. We all end up writing sections or paragraphs that we really like and we are really proud of, but sometimes they just don't fit in.

So what do you do? You take the advice once offered by another writer: "Murder your darlings."

This has been credited to several famous people over the years, but it is not really important to us who said it. It is more important to remember the meaning—that you should be prepared to get rid of those passages of writing which you particularly like, are often found to be self indulgent rather than having any particular use to anyone else.

If you are unsure about a section simply highlight it and carry on editing your eBook. You will benefit from going through the eBook two or three times before you publish it, because you are very likely to miss things during the review.

Fitting editing into your schedule

You might think that when you have actually written your eBook the hard work is complete, but there is still a lot of work. It's up to you to make sure you stay focused.

Rather than ripping up your writing schedule that has helped you so much up until this point (you'll need it again for your next eBook anyway, won't you?), keep a hold of it and simply change the name to your editing schedule. Simple! It's the easiest way to make sure you keep on going.

The benefits of reading it aloud

At the risk of appearing mad, I am going to ask you to read your eBook out loud.

You don't need an audience for this, although if you family members that you trust and who can give you constructive feedback without criticizing everything you have done, you might want to ask for help. Most writers will do this so make sure you have some quiet time where you either have the house to yourself or you won't be disturbed.

So why on earth should you read your eBook out loud?

Well, this might surprise you, but it is one of the best ways of making sure that you get the finished product to be as good as you can possibly make it.

You see, when you read something out loud, you will start to feel the rhythm of what you have written. I know that sounds a little odd.

It is true, however. If you read a paragraph out loud, you will immediately know if it works. Sometimes you will write something that you think sounds pretty good on the page. But when you read it out loud, your tongue trips over the words you have, and you start to stumble and have to go back and try to read it again.

If this happens, then you know the words aren't flowing as they should and you need to rewrite it. In fact, you can rephrase the sentence out loud until you find what works, and use that instead.

You may find after some practice, and after you have written a couple more eBooks that you don't have to do this anymore. Some writers automatically hear that voice in their head as they are writing, and they will instantly know whether the piece they are writing has that unmistakable rhythm that will carry a reader through from the beginning to the end.

This is a powerful technique; you just need to get use to hearing the sound of your own voice for a while!

Where does this information belong?

Editing is a skill just as writing is, and you will get better and more efficient the more you do. Although as you become a better writer, you should have less editing to do anyway!

But in this part of the chapter on editing I am going to go through a number of scenarios you might well come up against when you are editing your eBook. These examples should help you to figure out what you should do when you come across these particular situations yourself.

So let's take a look at them.

Should you think about the eBook structure now?

Structure is just as important when you are editing as it is while you are writing. During the editing process, you should keep a look out for evidence of your structure. Is it still there?

The best way to go about this is to keep your written outline next to you while you are editing your eBook. Read through the outline once again (print off another copy if you have scribbled all over it during the writing process, as I often do) before you tackle each chapter, and keep it in mind as you are reading each one.

Have you have been able to stick to the outline? If you have written a good outline and broken it down into bite sized chunks to begin with, you shouldn't find too many problems at this stage. It is actually harder to go off course than it is to stay on it!

It does happen though that you can read through your eBook and suddenly discover that your outline is nowhere to be found. What happened? Somewhere halfway through that chapter there your outline disappeared. It comes back again later on, but it completely went out the window there for a while.

If you find you have done this, take a moment to think about why. It is vitally important to find out why you have veered off your outline because one of the below things happened:

- Your deviation might be perfectly acceptable—it might actually have been called for in your outline but you missed it.

- Your deviation hasn't added to the eBook at all.

The first case scenario is a sign of good writing, so well done if you can honestly say this is the case! When you are planning any eBook you will find that you can brainstorm the idea and jot down notes and thoughts about all aspects of it... but it isn't until you start to write it and go into much more depth that a lot more ideas and possibilities occur to you. It's easy to miss something which has a rightful place in the finished eBook, so don't be afraid to include something like this should it happen.

The second case scenario isn't really a setback. All you need to do is cut out the part of the eBook that doesn't belong and keep it out of the finished version. Don't forget you may be able to use it elsewhere—perhaps there is another eBook in that idea? But if not... then it's time to 'murder your darling'.

This brings up the point of whether or not you should alter your structure at this late stage. You can only answer this question once you have read the entire eBook, but quite often there won't be any need to. You might need to add something to the original structure, as we have seen in the above example, but there shouldn't really be any need to alter it in any major fashion. Steer clear of hacking away at your eBook until there is nothing left to work with—and always, always, always keep an original copy somewhere just in case your file gets lost or corrupted. It's worth saying that more than once!

"Is that information in the right place?"

This is a classic problem that can occur with any type of eBook, no matter the subject.

When creating a rough outline which consists of only a few bullet points for each chapter or section, it can be difficult to see exactly what will go where.

You think you have got your head around your eBook and what will go where once you start unleashing all those ideas you've got flying around in your head. And then you start writing, and it doesn't quite seem as smooth a road as you thought it might be.

That's not a bad thing though. That's called writing. It's what happens when you realize how much there is underneath that framework you started out with. I think it was Stephen King who likened writing a story, fiction in his example, to digging up an artifact. The more you dig, the more you uncover. And it is just the same with your eBook, no matter what your topic.

If you come across information that you know should be included, but you're not sure where to put it, try making a shortlist of the places it could fit in. You might end up with three or four, but that's fine. Make a list of each starting with the earliest possible appearance first and the last appearance at the end.

Next, think about the first possibility and ask yourself what would happen if you didn't include that piece of information at that point. Would the eBook still make sense? Would your readers know what they were reading if you introduced it at some later stage instead?

Work through all the possibilities and see which place it fits in best. This method will usually reveal the right place for it. If it doesn't, include it in the first position, so long as it isn't completely out of place there. And of course if it is, it shouldn't be there anyway, right? You will soon get used to shuffling facts and nuggets of information around to get the best result.

Don't forget that you can always reintroduce information somewhere else later on by way of a reminder. You may also want to mention something early on, and elaborate on it in much more detail further on in the eBook.

For example, in this book I included a chapter very early on about the five most important things that all good eBooks have. Remember that one?

Well one of those five things was the need for the eBook to have its own mini-site to be sold from. Now the next chapter after this one is on that very subject, but of course I have already introduced it, so you know a little bit about it already.

That's good because I have already planted the seed for your next stage.

Next, we will go into a lot more detail, and I will reveal more about how to actually get that mini-site up and running. So instead of just having the bare bones of what is needed, you will know everything.

This example of mentioning something once and then elaborating on it later can be used to excite readers, tempt them into staying with you, and let them know that there is more to come. For example, I could tell you here that chapter fourteen is going to tell you how to promote your eBook once you have written, edited and published it... but you won't find out exactly how you can do that until you get to that chapter!

These techniques combine with your writing technique to make sure that you are going to have a great eBook. You will see how they come into play in your sales page for your eBook as well—that's still to come.

What about punctuation?

If you don't pay attention to punctuation you could end up getting stuck on a train of thought that just keeps on going in much the same way as it would in your brain and it doesn't always become obvious straightaway that you've kept on going just to get the whole thought down on paper and there is no sign of a full stop or even a comma in sight.

Whew. Try reading that sentence again in a single breath! With punctuation it is much easier to read and understand.

You can see why punctuation is so important. Long sentences are fine, but don't expect your readers to be able to remember what you were talking about at the beginning. In fact the chances are good that you won't remember either. Short sentences are fine too, and they help to mix things up a bit as well.

Remember what I said earlier about the need to make sure your read your eBook out loud before you publish it? This technique will help you decide whether or not you have punctuated properly.

How long are your paragraphs?

Are they a mile long or do they consist of a single sentence on a regular basis? There is nothing wrong with single sentence paragraphs—you'll notice I have used a few in this book. They can have more impact when they stand apart from the sentences on either side.

You also need to think about cutting out really long paragraphs. The longer a paragraph goes on for, the much less likely it is that your readers will stick with it. There is no hard and fast rule as to how many lines the maximum length should run to, but don't overdo it.

Readers like to see lots of little chunks they can read. Gone are the days when novels could be published with paragraphs that went on for pages and pages without a break.

Nice and short. That's the way your readers will like it. And don't forget you can break them up with images too, should you decide to use them.

More editing tips

A great way to read your work for the "first time" is to read in reverse. If you never heard of this great tip you will quickly learn the value of this tip. This technique forces you to bypass the brain's habit of filling in what it thinks it will see.

Rather than adding to your content to make a point more clearly, try cutting out words and making the remaining words more concise. Writers are overly wordy, especially when writing non-fiction. Straight forward and concise writing should be your goal.

Question every sentence and word why it is included? If there is no reason, then delete it. Sentences and words that do not provide value must be deleted to the recycle bin.

Don't say things over and over again, say it once and move on. This is a waste of your time and your reader's time. Say it once concisely and move on. For example, "focus your attention on this" is the same as "focus on this".

Don't write passive sentences. Avoid "to be" (and its conjugations is, was, were, are, am) as these are indicators that the sentence is passive, which means the subject is acted upon rather than doing the acting. Passive sentences are weak and are not convincing to the reader. For example, "We were sliding down the hill like a rocket" compared to "Jane and I rocketed down the hill." The later is more believable, exciting, and concise.

Use adverbs conservatively as they often pad/fatten/stretch a sentence unnecessarily. For example, "Jane and I rocketed quickly down the hill." Don't insult your readers; assume they know what rocketed means.

How to find qualified people to review your eBook

Now it is time for another point of view. Ask family and friends to read your eBook and provide feedback. That reminds me, thanks Dad!

What makes complete sense to you may confuse others so it is a good idea to incorporate comments and suggestions.

This is also a good time to find a member of the family or friend with a firm grip on the English language to edit your eBook. Make certain that they use the Track Changes tool in MS Word so that you can review their edits and accept or decline them as you deem necessary.

How to find a pro to edit your eBook

Another option for editing your eBook is to use the freelance websites such as www.elance.com and www.guru.com to hire an editor. You may be surprised at how economical this service can be. If you are offering your book in print, you can also consider the editing services offered by www.booksurge.com or www.lulu.com, which are usually a little more expensive.

How do you know when you have finished?

Writing and editing an eBook is much like creating a painting. You could carry on painting a work of art for years if you wanted to, constantly adding a touch of color here and there, but never quite finishing it.

You need to decide when it is the best that you can make it. At some point you have to let it go, otherwise it will never get to market.

You will learn when to let it go, and when you have done the best job you can. Self publishing does makes things a little harder in this respect. If you were publishing a physical book through a traditional publishing house, you would have your own editor who would help you write the best book you could—and he/she would be with you every step of the way.

The best way to determine if your eBook is complete is to go to your favorite internet marketing forum and send a private message to a senior member that is respected by the community and has a history of offering helpful posts throughout the forum. Be humble. Ask this member if they know anyone he/she respects who would be interested in reviewing your eBook in return for a free review copy.

With luck this person will offer to look it over for you and provide comments. They will likely only give it a quick scan as their time is limited, but they can tell you if the eBook is ready, or if it is only 70% complete. The information they provide can be invaluable, so take constructive criticism as it was intended, to help you. This can save you a lot of embarrassment. Just think what would happen if you launched a product that you thought was complete, only to find that your market considers your product inferior. Your reputation will be soundly damaged.

You can also let your target market tell you if the eBook is ready. You can create a survey, for free, and use survey monkey (and other survey services) to ask several questions about your eBook. You can ask customers about the quality of the content, the price, the writing and flow, etc. This can be done by doing a pre-launch where you put a link to your survey in the footer of your eBook (this footer link is temporary during pre-launch) and offer the readers a $5 cash back offer payable through PayPal upon completion of the survey. You can also advertise this cash back program to help generate sales.

You can use PayPal to process payments, including credit cards, on your mini-site during the pre-launch stage. Remember, this is a pre-launch and the goal of the finished eBook will be to sell thousands of copies on affiliate networks, like ClickBank (more on that later).

About second editions (and third and fourth...)

If you are having doubts about when to let go of your eBook and publish it to the waiting public you can publish the eBook as a first edition, and then publish an updated version in the future, but that doesn't give you the green light to publish an inferior eBook.

It does mean that if you have written an eBook that has many web addresses and online information in it (which as we all know changes by the minute), you can offer a new updated version later.

A benefit of a frequently updating eBook gives you an opportunity to communicate with your former customer by sending them an email about the updated eBook. You can include advertising, affiliate links, or your own product links with the update email to generate some extra cash.

If you like this idea, you should charge more for the initial eBook with free updates to buyers. That will produce more money per sale, and it will cover the amount of work you need to do at future stages. Remember that you're selling an advanced product due to those updates.

If you choose this method, you must plan for those updates in advance. When are you going to do them? It's no good making a big thing of it in your sales letter if you never get around to doing it. Planning the updated version for, say, six months after the original eBook comes out is a good idea, with another update six months after that.

This method may not work for every eBook you write, but some will certainly benefit from it. This can be particularly true for eBooks that are related in some way to earning money online, since the landscape of internet marketing is constantly changing. You may recommend a certain method which is perfectly workable now, but ends up being superseded by something else in a month. With an updated version you can add this in, perhaps by writing a new chapter to include with the eBook.

Conclusion

Some people find editing boring, but it's worthwhile to ensure you give your customers the best possible product possible. Regardless of how tricky and boring you find it, you must persevere to create a professional product.

If you can do that, you will soon be publishing a much better eBook than you thought you were capable of. And that will bring you more repeat customers for your second and subsequent eBooks in the future.

Chapter 7:
Selling Your EBook with a Website

You'll remember that we touched on this in the first chapter as one of the top five things all good eBooks have. Selling your eBook through a website is just as important as writing the eBook. Websites that only sell one eBook and focus completely on persuading visitors to purchase the eBook are mini-sites. You tell people know how darn good this eBook really is! Think of it as the difference between sticking a copy of your book on the back shelf in a bookshop... or putting a big display of them just inside the door, with a big billboard outside telling everyone that it's there.

You've got to blow your own trumpet in this business; otherwise you won't make many sales. That's a fact. So be proud of your eBook and make sure that you shout about it at the top of your lungs.

Why a dedicated website?

If you hadn't seen any before, I am sure that by now you will have looked online and come across plenty of eBooks that are being sold from a dedicated mini-site. This is by far the best way to sell them since the only focus is on one eBook.

If you want to write and sell ten eBooks in the next year or two you need to plan this process in advance. How much is that going to cost you in domain names and hosting fees for ten separate mini-sites? Surely it will be a whole lot cheaper to stick them all on one larger website—especially if all the eBooks are on similar subjects?

Those extra fees can be covered with one or two eBook sales for each mini-site, so it is worth the extra cost. You can also get a domain name and web hosting very inexpensively nowadays. Depending on the web package you choose, there will either be a limit to the number of websites you can host, or it will be unlimited.

That means that if you bought the unlimited package, you could literally write a hundred separate eBooks and set up a mini-site for each one—and they would all be hosted under the terms of that one package. And the price for this kind of service is a lot less than you might think.

One of the main problems with putting everything on one website is that it makes things harder for people to find. Let's start with the domain name for example. If you have a mini-site for each eBook, then your domain name can relate directly to that specific eBook.

With a single domain per eBook that focuses on a single product, you can use keywords and phrases that directly relate to your eBook. For example, if you wrote an eBook on how golfers can lower their scores you would want to consider domain names such as www.loweryourgolfscorein30days.com or www.lowergolfscores.com

Choosing a domain name

The number one rule here is to choose carefully; because a good domain name will help you rank higher in the search engines. Short domain names work best, but you should try and use either the complete title of your eBook or a segment of it that makes sense and includes relevant keywords relating to the subject of your eBook. It will get you organic traffic (i.e. free) from the search engines.

What else should you consider when you are thinking about which domain name to go for?

It's worth reiterating what I said much earlier about sticking to the .com suffix when you choose your domain name. The .com suffix is regarded as being a global website, and since you are selling eBooks you will want to make sure that people have no doubts about the global appeal of your eBook.

If you use a .co.uk name, or a .com.au name, or any other variation, then people might make the wrong assumption that your eBook is only written for people in those countries. Worse still, they might assume it is a tangible paperback book, and you will only mail it to people in your own country.

So go global and make sure everyone knows they are welcome to buy a copy.

Hyphen or no hyphen?

Before you rush into choosing a domain name, think about how it will look.

One of the biggest questions that people ask is whether they should put hyphens in between the words the domain name is made of. Of course this only applies if you have more than one word in between the www. and the .com parts.

For example www.example.com doesn't need hyphens anyway. But what about www.thisisanexample.com? What would you do there? Would www.this-is-an-example.com be better?

There is no right or wrong answer to this, but I know which one I prefer. If you want to know which one I hate the most, try typing those two web addresses out right now on your keyboard. Which one is the faster one to type? And which one takes ages and usually results in you having to hunt your way around the keyboard to type it in?

For my money I wouldn't use hyphens because it makes the web address look very long and clunky. And if you take a look at plenty of big name businesses online, you will find that the majority of them don't use hyphens either.

And it's not just because of the hassle it creates in typing it into the address bar in your browser either. Let's say you're talking to someone about your website and they want to know what the address is. Which one of the following things would you rather say?

1. "Oh yes, my website is called www dot this is an example dot com...", or

2. "Oh yes, my website is called www dot this hyphen is hyphen a hyphen example dot com..."

My guess is that if you had chosen the second example, they would have walked away halfway through you trying to get the sentence out!

The moral here is that you should always write down your domain name and say it out loud before you actually buy it. If you don't, you might regret it later on. About the only time that a hyphen is okay is if you only have two words in your domain name. Then it can work, but if you can get away without them, you're better off doing so.

Watch out for weird spellings

This is another compulsion that some people seem to have, but it can really backfire on you.

You have probably seen websites where the name of the company ends in a z instead of an s. For example, they might spell the word toys with a 'z' instead of an 's'.

Weird and unusual spellings might catch the eye, but they don't usually make websites easy to find. If you are searching for toys, which word are you going to type into your search engine? Toys or toyz?

But you shouldn't use them in the domain name. Some major businesses may get away with it if it is part of their brand, but on the whole, you should give yourself the best possible chance of getting found online.

Tips for buying a great domain name

Register your domain name at one of the popular domain registration websites. Make the domain as short as possible with your keyword/phrase and use a Top Level Domain. The best real estate on the internet is and always will be .com, so consider this when buying a domain name.

The practice of adding hyphens to a domain name is still being debated.

Pros include:

- Easier to obtain a domain name as hyphens increase the number of possibilities using the same key phrase.

- Potentially better for Search Engine Optimization (SEO) as the hyphen clearly separates the keywords to reduce the possibility that the search engines confuse your keywords. This possibility is greatly reduced with the ever improving search engine software.

Cons include:

- Difficult to communicate a domain with hyphens. Imagine telling someone to go to NewMarketHurricanes.com compared to new-market-hurricanes.com.

- Considered less important and sometimes spammy by many people.

- Longer domain with hyphens.

- Increased number of available domains when using numbers with your keywords, but it can add confusion to search engines (is it 1 or one?), and it rarely "rolls off the tongue" or is memorable.

Below is a step by step guide to setting up your domain name, hosting account, and blog. Instructions are based on the more popular providers of each service.

Go to www.godaddy.com, or your favorite domain registration company, and register your domain name. Set the nameservers to point to the webhosting service that you select. You can add the two nameservers by clicking the "Add Nameservers while checking out of GoDaddy.

Setting up webhosting steps

Go to www.hostgator.com, www.ultrawebsitehosting.com, or your favorite hosting company, and set up an Ultra Hosting Plan or an Ultra Reseller Plan. The Reseller Plan gives you 10 GBs of disk space and 400 GBs for as many websites as you wish, and it is quite simple to use. Bookmark the log in URL so that it is easy to find in the future.

Most webhosting companies use cPanel for control panel management. Click "Create New Account" and add your new domain name and assign it about 200MB disk space.

There are many great books on WordPress that will help you with your blog. To get you started you can automatically install the WordPress blogging platform go to cPanel and click on Fantastico Deluxe icon located directly below the "Web Host Manager."

Click on WordPress and:

- Click "Add New Installation" in box on right.

- Fill in information required. If you wish the blog to be on the homepage of the domain that you purchased (i.e. www.mynewdomain.com) then leave the second box empty. If you wish to add it to www.mynewblog.com/blog then only type the blog into the second box.

- Fill in the remaining information required. You may want to consider using the same username and password and email address for all blogs, as things can get confusing as you ramp up to be a prolific blogger.

- Click on "Install WordPress."

- Click "Finish Installation."

- Type in your email address and click "Send Email."

- TIP: You can watch 29 free how-to videos on using cPanel at www.viralprofitautomator.com/videos.

- You can now go to your blogs URL and click on Log In icon under Meta in the right hand navigation bar.

- In the WordPress Dashboard click on "Settings" and go to the "General" section and set the tagline, date/time, and permalinks (to use real URLs based on the posts names rather than an odd ending such as .com/?p1943).

- In the WordPress Dashboard use the Help, Forum, and Plugins sections to learn everything that you need about using the program.

So should I promote my products on my blog?

Let's make this clear right now. Your blog can be used to promote your eBook, but it shouldn't just be used for that. The idea is almost to promote subliminally, without your readers knowing that you're even doing it.

If you made every post about a different product you sell, ending it with a link to buy that product from your main website, then you shouldn't expect very good results. People will see it for what it is—a promotional blog existing only to plug products that are already being advertised and sold elsewhere.

No, the purpose of a blog is to engage your audience and let them get to know you and what you do, in more detail and depth. The internet can be a very impersonal place and blogs help to knock down some of the walls that exist between you and your potential customers. By engaging and communicating with people through your blog posts, they will naturally become more interested in you, and will click through to your eBook mini-site on their own terms.

How could we promote those eBooks without doing so directly?

Here's how. You would create a category in your blog where you write about your eBooks topic, so you could blog about it on a regular basis. You could share some of your own experiences about earning money from selling eBooks on your website, and invite comments from readers to get them more involved in your blog as well. And at the end of these posts you could direct the readers with a call to action using a link to your eBook mini-site. Your goal with the blog is to offer valuable information and build trust with your readers, which is called pre-selling.

You wouldn't directly ask them to buy anything on your blog (your eBook mini-site sales page will do that), and you wouldn't pre-sell them as such either; what you are doing is sharing your knowledge on the subject of earning money from selling eBooks, and basically saying 'Hey look, there's more information on this subject on my other website…'

People don't like a strong sell—it turns them off and they end up doing the exact opposite of what you wanted them to do. But by taking the time to help them out and provide useful information on your blog, you are developing a relationship of trust with them that will be much more likely to result in a sale of your current eBook and possibly your future ones also.

You may have heard of something called a 'call to action' being the most important aspect of any website, mini-site, sales page, article, and blog posting. A call to action is the most important thing you want a reader to do before they leave you're the webpage they are at. So for example it could be to:

- Buy a product
- Sign up for a mailing list
- Request a free report
- Visit your main eBook mini-site sales page

… and any one of a dozen other things, although the above four are the top choices.

Your call to action on your blog may simply be to get the reader interested enough in what you are talking about to click through to your eBook mini-site. You could set up a free report about earning money from eBooks and give it to people visiting your blog. You would require an email address to access the free report and this will build an email list that you can market to in the future. Every page of your free report would have your eBook mini-site address on it (point to the sales page).

How much control do you want over your blog?

You have likely noticed that there are plenty of providers out there who are willing to let you have your own blog hosted on their network completely free of charge.

Isn't that great?

Not necessarily. You see, most things that are free come with certain restrictions, and free blogs are no exception. The main problem is that the vast majority of them don't like you to promote anything in your blog. There are very precise rules that need to be followed and if you fall foul of any of them, you could well try to log into your blog one day only to find it isn't there any more. If this happens, you've got no recourse and no way of getting it back—and half the time the blog network involved won't even respond to your emails.

It also gives you a much more professional look and feel. After all you're a business, so you should be able to afford the relatively small cost of hosting your own blog online. At least that is what your customers will think. If you really are stuck for cash initially, then start off with a free blog—but transfer it to your own hosting package as soon as you possibly can.

Get linking!

The purpose of having a blog is to drive quality traffic (traffic that has an interest in your eBook subject) to your eBook mini-site. You should use linking to raise the profile of your blog and your eBook mini-site.

What is linking all about anyway?

Let's start by looking at the different types of linking you should be using as often as possible:

- Linking different pages within a website or blog - this helps search engine spiders to find their way around a website and gets more pages into the search engine results. Be sure to add a link to you home page on every page on your website. The link text should be the title of the website, not "Home."

- Linking from your blog or website to other websites - you want to link to sales pages of products that you sell on other websites. You may also want to include a few affiliate links throughout the blog to point to related product sales pages when appropriate.

- Linking from other websites to your blog or website - this will raise your search engine ranking. Link to your blog from the signature line in your emails, from your website, and from any social networking websites you belong to. It is well worth the effort to search out forums that have a high page rank and are directly related to your niche. Join these forums and introduce yourself in the "Introduce Yourself" section that most forums have (don't mention your product or blog yet, you need to build a bit of a reputation first). Then post useful and meaningful comments where possible. Set up your signature as soon as possible. Some of the higher quality forums require you to make a certain number of posts prior to setting up a signature. Be sure to include a link to your blog and your sales page and include a good "hook" to entice people to follow your links.

Do not ignore linking, because over time it can really work in your favor, bringing you a higher search engine ranking and more customers and traffic as well, <u>for free</u>.

Linking from other websites to your own blog is harder, but that is where the next chapter comes in. You will soon find out about a neat method for creating as many links coming back to your blog (and your website, if you so desire) as you want!

The number one blogging rule

Blogging for publicity is more of a slow burner method than the quick results you'll gain from sending out a well targeted press release.

But in no way does that mean you should give up on it if you're not getting the results you want.

While some blogs get great results right from the beginning, the vast majority of successful ones develop over time to become the success stories they are today. So persevere and remember that you are blogging to make yourself and your business better known.

And with each and every blog post you write, you'll be doing just that.

Chapter 8: Mini-site Design and Sample Content

A mini-site is not just a single sales page with a buy now button. Search engines like websites that provide valuable content and they don't usually consider a single page website as valuable and will likely rank that type of website low in search results (i.e. no free traffic from search engines). Another issue with a single page website is Google slams these websites with poor AdWords Quality Scores, which results in higher advertising costs when using Google AdWords.

Google explains Quality Score as "The AdWords system calculates a 'Quality Score' for each of your keywords. It looks at a variety of factors to measure how relevant your keyword is to your ad text and to a user's search query. A keyword's Quality Score updates frequently and is closely related to its performance. In general, a high Quality Score means that your keyword will trigger ads in a higher position and at a lower cost-per-click (CPC)."

The navigation links (i.e. Homepage, About Us, Contact Us, Privacy Policy, and so on) should be located in an inconspicuous area on your home/sales page to prevent taking attention away from the reader. The typical location is on the bottom of the mini-site in the footer. The pages each every mini-site should have are described below. These are the minimum number of pages you need for your mini-site.

Free Privacy Policy Page text

Privacy Policy - A professional mini-site should have a privacy policy, and that will keep Google happy, so spend a few minutes and post one on your mini-site and link to it from your sales page at the bottom in your mini-site footer. You can move the navigation bar anywhere you like on the rest of the pages within the mini-site, but keep it out of sight on the sales page so that you don't distract the reader from acting on your call to action. You can use a privacy policy offered free at www.tele-pro.co.uk/pages/legal/privacy.htm or you can modify one for your specific mini-site to meet Google requirements at www.macuha.com/privacy-policy. If you plan to use this policy, I recommend that you capture the screen shot showing that the website owner is offering the use of his policy and keep it filed for your own protection.

Free Disclaimer Page text

Disclaimer - If you are promoting a product that claims that you have made money using this product or that your buyer will make money with your product, you need an earnings disclaimer. For a starting point, you can use the information at www.tele-pro.co.uk/pages/legal/terms.htm#Disclaimer.

FAQ Page sample text

FAQ - ClickBank requires sellers provide specific information to buyers, and this can be accomplished with the FAQ page on your mini-site. It also provides information that will help buyers access your product. You are welcome to use the FAQ that I created:

Q. What name will I see on my credit card statement?

A. Your credit card or bank statement will show a charge by CLKBANK*COM or Clk*Bank.com for this purchase.

Q. Can I make the purchase without a credit card?

A. You can use a credit card or PayPal to make payment.

Q. What is an eBook?

A. An eBook, or electronic book, is a 100% digital product that you will download to your computer. The eBook can be read on the computer, much like reading a Word or WordPerfect document. The eBook is in an eBook format called PDF and requires Adobe Reader. This software is available free of charge here. For more information and tips on using Adobe Reader please click here.

Q. I am having trouble using my credit card, what may be the problem?

A. You may wish to set up a PayPal account using your credit card or bank account. Once set up, you should be able to make the purchase through ClickBank, just select PayPal as the form of payment. For more information, visit *www.paypal.com.*

Q. What free ongoing information can I expect to receive?

A. You will receive a monthly newsletter full of valuable information to keep you up to date on the latest information available on this topic.

Q. What if I have any concerns with my purchase?

A. If you have any problems with your purchase, you can email us. We usually respond within three hours. Please remember to include your phone number in your email, so that we can follow up with a phone call.

Q. How do I get my eBook and files?

A. Click on the download link. Once the product is downloaded, the software WinZip will open with the files in it. Click on the "Extract" icon and select a location on your computer, such as your desktop, to extract the files. This is similar to saving your files, so once complete you can go to the location where you saved the files to start using your products. Yes. To open many of the below compressed files, you will need to use WinZip. A free 45-day trial is available with easy to follow step by step instructions on how to use the WinZip. The software can be found at *www.winzip.com*.

Q. When will I receive my eBook and related products?

A. The eBook and related products will be available immediately after the payment is complete. You will automatically be taken to the download page.

Q. I didn't download the products right way and now I don't know what the web address (or URL) was. Where can I find the download page?

A. The download page URL was emailed to you when you made the purchase. Click on the link in the email or copy and paste it into your web browser and it will take you to the download page. WARNING: The download page is only available for 24 hours after your purchase, so please download ASAP. Please feel free to contact us if you have an issue, and we will be happy to assist you.

Q. Is the eBook available as a hard copy?

A. There will be a hard copy book in the coming months, so watch for it at www.YourWebsite.com and your favorite book store.

Q. Can I print my eBook for easier reading?

A. Yes. You can click on "File" and then "Print" and select your printer, or click on the printer icon.

Q. What currency do you accept?

A. We accept most currencies. Your credit card will pay in US Dollars and will convert the funds on your credit card. To determine the cost in your currency, you can go to *http://www.oanda.com/convert/classic* and follow the instructions.

Q. Can I share the eBook with friends?

A. The eBook is protected by the United States Copyrighting Laws. The eBook is protected with a security feature that does not permit the document to be emailed. The eBook may be printed for the buyer's personal use. The eBook cannot be posted on the internet and may not be made available via download or any other method.

Q. I am having technical issues, can someone help me?

A. Please feel free to email support, and we will get back to you shortly, usually within three hours during business hours (9am - 5pm EST). Please include the receipt number and "Technical Support" in the subject line of your email. Also, please accurately describe the issue, so that we can work to resolve it immediately.

Affiliate Sign-Up Page

Affiliate sign-up page - This is the page where you will be sending potential affiliates in order to convince them to sign up to promote your product. Therefore, this is also a sales page, though much smaller than your sales page. You should set up an account with an auto responder such as www.getresponse.com or www.aweber.com to capture affiliate names and email addresses, which will allow you to contact them when you have new affiliate tools, product updates, milestones, etc. to share with your affiliate team.

Although ClickBank manages commission tracking and payments to affiliates, the professionals use additional affiliate management software where you can sell multiple ClickBank products from one ClickBank account (pays for itself after a few products). I use easy-ClickMate, a ClickBank Affiliate Management Tool found at www.easybiztools.com. This software manages the affiliate tools page, automatically notifies affiliates of sales, and provides statistical analytics. The most important benefit of this software, in my option, is that your affiliates have to sign up to access the affiliate tools, so you have their name and email address which enables you to communicate with them about current and future products.

Affiliate tools example

Affiliate tools page - This is your opportunity to help your affiliates with their promotion campaign. The quality and quantity of tools you provide to your affiliates will affect how many affiliates sign up and promote your product. You should have your mini-site designer require that the affiliates use their ClickBank nickname for their users name to log into auto responder and automatically populate their ClickBank nickname into all the affiliate tools that you offer. This will save your affiliates time and they will appreciate that.

You should also host your affiliate banners on your own servers and provide the code to your affiliates so that your server space is used to serve up banner ads rather than using your affiliate server space. Many affiliates are concerned with the amount of bandwidth they use each month.

Contact Us Page

The contact us page should be a form that the customer submits to your admin or support email address. The customers should have to submit their names, email addresses, and comments/questions in the form, then you will receive them in your email inbox. This method will reduce the amount of spam that you receive from programs scraping your email addresses off your webpage. Your web designer can handle this easily for you.

"Blog" - If you have a blog that promotes your product on another domain name, you will want to include a link to it.

Sales Page

Sales page - The sales page is likely your home page. Of the many things you and your web designer will need to consider is the colors you will be using on the mini-site. Color makes a big impression on the reader and certain colors refer to certain things, such as red with excitement and anger, green with money, and blue with confidence. Make certain your colors project the feelings that you wish to portray. There is a good chance that your web designer is also a graphics designer or knows one and can recommend a color scheme for your product and target market. Try to stick to no more than three or four colors.

If you look at a typical mini-site, you will notice that there is a background of some kind—quite often plain in a single color, or graded in several shades of that color. The most common background is a light solid color, or no color at all other than the border. This is to prevent the reader from being distracted from the sales page copy.

The sales letter itself sits in the middle of the screen, so that there is effectively a border on all sides. This draws the eyes inward to focus on the text in the middle of the page. Sales page copy (text) is narrower than regular websites. Think about newspapers, why do you think they use narrow columns? Because they hold the readers attention longer! See chapters nine and ten for more information on sales pages.

ClickBank Thank You Page

When a buyer purchases your product they are redirected to your Thank You page where he or she will download your eBook and bonuses. ClickBank has a few requirements that must be met for product approval, including a support email address, the name on buyer credit card statements, and a link to another page. An example follows:

"Congratulations on buying my eBook. I'm sure you will be delighted with your purchase and I thank you for your support. Please remember that your credit card or bank statement will show a charge by ClickBank, CLKBANK*COM, or Clk*Bank.com for this purchase.

Your bonuses may be downloaded with the below links together with your eBook and audio file and your first newsletter will be arriving in your inbox very soon!

Good luck, and enjoy reading the book.

To open many of the below compressed files you will need to use WinZip. A free 45-day trial is available here and instructions on how to use the WinZip software are here ("here" will be your links).

You will also need Acrobat Reader to open the eBook and that is available free here. For more information and tips on using Adobe Reader please click here.

If you have any problems with your order you may contact us at support@mydomain.com and we usually respond within a few hours."

Adding security to your mini-site

Unfortunately internet marketers have to deal with unsavory people who will find a way to download your products for free. Some of these people will actually post your product in free download websites where hundreds or thousands may score free copies.

The best way to protect you and your affiliates is to use a software add on such as www.easyclickguard.com or www.dlguard.com/dlginfo/index.php.

Making sure it all blends in

Making sure it all blends in extends from the point I made about color. The idea is that your background color and your sales letter should all pull together and form a cohesive and attractive looking mini-site for people to look at.

This type of mini-site usually has a headline which screams out at people from the top of the page. It will be in larger, bolder type than the rest of the sales letter, and it will normally be in the same color (or at least a different shade of it) as the background. When the reader arrives on your sales page, they still have their finger hovering over their mouse, ready to click away. You only have about four seconds to grab the reader's attention before they click away, so make the most of your main headline.

Chapter 9: Sales Page Optimization

Another good way of blending everything in is to put additional pieces of information that you need to have in your sales page in boxes which have that same color border around them. These are other ways of making sure the whole thing hangs together nicely.

As we progress further and you learn how to write a great sales letter that will sell more copies of your eBook, you will recognize the areas of the sales letter that will benefit from being displayed in this way. We have plenty more to learn yet, but by the end of this chapter you will know how to promote your eBook to the best of your ability through your mini-site. And you will also know how to use all the best techniques available to ensure that people are clamoring to buy it.

Focus on the first screen full of information

This applies to what you write for your sales page as well, but I am going to mention it here because it applies to the design as well.

When someone visits your mini-site, what is the first thing they are going to see?

The top of your mini-site sales page.

That means you must make sure that top section is absolutely engaging to entice the reader to learn more about what you have to say. You must ensure that everyone who sees it is going to feel compelled to start scrolling down to see what else you have to say.

You can achieve a lot with carefully chosen words here, and we will cover that in a moment, but you can also do a lot with images. These are, after all, the first things that someone will see.

So look at the title of your eBook very carefully. What images does it bring to mind? For example, let's take the title of this book you're reading now and see what images we get:

"Make Money Online: Write and Sell EBooks Guide A Home Business That is Easy to Start"

What does this bring to mind?

Here is what I came up with:

- **It's about eBooks.** So a pile of books perhaps? Or more likely, since this is all about eBooks as opposed to paperback books, a picture of a computer with a graphic of a book or a stack of pages coming out of it.

- **Home based business.** Most people think about working from home at some time or another, so what images could there be that encapsulate that? The idea of working with our feet up, tapping away at a laptop placed on our knees—that could work. It fits in with the idea of writing eBooks on the computer as well. We could mock up the picture to include a view over the person's shoulder, so we can see they are writing a document of some kind.

- **Money.** This one is simple. Stacks of cash perhaps. Or even better, someone sitting among piles of banknotes. How about someone sitting at their computer (we would have the viewpoint of sitting behind the screen, looking directly at the person), with a stream of banknotes coming out of the computer screen? There are loads of possibilities here.

- **Internet.** Once again, this would probably involve a computer screen. Perhaps with a browser window open and someone looking at a sales page of a brand new eBook?

You can see how it's perfectly possible to start generating ideas for images without doing anything more than looking at the title of your eBook. In fact, it's probably completely unnecessary to do anything else, since people will take in two things when they land on your mini-site sales page—the images they see on that first screen full of information, and the words you put on there.

People react strongly to images, so you want to make sure you have one built into the header at the top of the screen. If you can show them an image that has positive connotations linked to what the eBook can do for them, you will be starting on a very positive footing indeed.

So you can see how important it is to concentrate on your design, especially where the first screen you see is concerned. Of course the writing on the sales page is the most important aspect of all, and we will be moving on to that in a moment.

But first let's consider a very important point in the creation of your mini-site.

D.I.Y. mini-site—or pay someone else?

There are two types of people out there today. The ones who know how to build a good mini-site and the ones that don't.

That might sound a little harsh, but it's true. And it's also a fact that a lot of the people who do know how to do it will charge the people who don't a nice fat fee to do it for them.

It's small wonder then that a lot of people consider whether or not they could do it on their own. It's tempting to muddle through and try to create web pages that do everything you want them to do, learning the ropes as you go along. But it isn't always the best way to go about things.

Mini-sites have only about five or six pages, so creating one is easier than creating a fifty page website! There are mini-site graphic packages which provide all the templates and instruction you need to build a decent and professional looking site for a low one-time fee, not including your domain name and hosting costs. But you will still be on your own to put the package together, which can be very tricky for those without experience building websites.

The biggest advantage in hiring a professional designer is they will complete the product much faster than you while producing a high end mini-site, which would likely be a challenge for you. You just give them the copy for each webpage on the mini-site, and a rough idea of what you want it to look like and the theme you are going for.

That can save you a lot of time, and as they same "time is money". Your time may be better spent on writing another eBook.

Chapter 10: Writing Sizzling Sales Page Copy

If you can write a great sales page that converts more than two sales per 100 people who visit your sales page, you will make money. If you can't, you may want to consider hiring an expert copyrighter, which will run you between $300 and $30,000. Obviously you get what you pay for with this large range of prices. The less expensive option is to drive more traffic to your mini-site to increase the number of sales each day. If you want to write you own sales page copy, you will need to learn the tips, tricks, and strategies.

Focus on length

Although the sales page is just a single page, you'll notice that many of them are quite long. This is to draw people in and tell them a story and all about the benefits of how your product will cure their "problem". The longer you can keep them on your sales page. The more chance you have of selling them your eBook, so you need to ensure that every single word you write is as good as you can possibly make it.

Do your research and look at some sales pages created for similar products being sold by other people. Don't copy them, but pay attention to what works and what really draws you in, and model yours on the same kind of format. You should be able to highlight and copy and paste the text on a page and insert it into a blank Word document to find out the amount of words that have been used to create the whole page. Do remember that you shouldn't edit or rewrite anyone else's web pages though—we're just using them here to get an idea of how long they are. It's far quicker than counting all the words individually!

I've experimented with quite a few sales pages, and the average length is around 3,000 words. The harder the product to sell and the more skeptical your target market, the longer the sales page will need to be to convince the reader to purchase your eBook.

So you can see that writing the sales page takes time to ensure that every single reader is convinced of how good the eBook is. And every single word must count.

What makes your eBook different?

Let's say you researched a subject and found that it was very popular. People were always searching for information about it, and there were plenty of eBooks out there already that dealt with the topic in one way or another. Ironically, even though you had all that competition, it told you that it was a popular topic, and it was something that you could write and sell books about.

This is where some people fail. They assume that they can write a great book on the subject, and it will sell really well without them having to work too hard on it. But of course it doesn't work like that. They might sell some copies, sure... but they won't sell anywhere near as many as they would if they could stand up and tell everyone what made their eBook special and what made it different from all the rest on that same topic.

Think about what your eBook includes and make sure you focus on that one thing that makes it unique. You can bet that people will be asking themselves this very same question when they are reading your sales page, and if you can tell them right up front what they are looking for, they will thank you for it and might even reward you with an order as well.

Another point you need to be aware of here is that you should be telling them more than once about that special something that sets your eBook apart from others. Don't tell them right up front and then assume they will remember for the rest of the sales page. They might, but regardless of whether they do or not, you need to be reminding them how fantastic your eBook is and why they need to buy your eBook instead of someone else's.

Make sure you are positive and encouraging

It's your job to lift the reader up and make them believe that getting your eBook will change their lives in some way.

It's obvious that no eBook can do that without help from the readers; they will need to put in their bit of effort too of course. You could give them the winning lottery numbers for next week... but they would still need to physically go out and buy a ticket.

It can help enormously to make a list of the points you want to get across during the course of your sales letter. So, for example, a eBook about earning a good income from writing eBook might cover these points:

- You can make a good second income from this venture.

- You can become a recognized author.

- You can become an expert on a particular subject that you love.

- You could build a whole new business that will result in replacing your current job altogether.

- Once the eBooks are written, you can carry on earning from them forever more.

- It can develop into a real 'hands off' business. The website is up 24/7, and you can set it up so that people can pay and receive their eBook straightaway, all without you having to do a thing.

- You can build up an income alongside your current job—so it's a safe thing to do.

- It's a very low cost business to get started in, unlike others which require an investment of thousands of dollars.

- You'll see a profit far more quickly than you would in many other businesses.

It's your job to make sure that you let them know just what your eBook can do for them. Don't be shy and pull back from telling them all the benefits your eBook has. Remember that doing all you can to promote your eBook will make the difference between no sales and lots of sales.

Now it could be that your product has one or two negative points—or at least, one or two points that could be construed as being negative when viewed in comparison with the competition.

For example, supposing someone else has released an eBook on the same subject that comes with a number of free videos as well. These videos actually show the readers how to complete certain steps and techniques that are included in the eBook. And let's further suppose that this particular eBook is already selling very well.

But yours doesn't have any of that. So what do you do?

It's simple. Don't make any reference at all to this other eBook, and don't say that yours doesn't have videos with it either. If you ever find yourself typing something negative when you are writing your sales page, edit it out immediately and turn it into a positive.

Don't focus on the negatives about your eBook for any reason. For example, your eBook might only be twenty pages long, and you might think that some people could look at that as being a negative point. They might not buy it for that reason. Maybe they're looking for something a lot longer and a lot meatier.

So what do you do?

Well to start with, you need to understand that just because an eBook is short, that doesn't mean that it is any less worthy than some of the longer eBooks being sold online today. In fact, I'll bet that many of the shorter ones are much better than the long ones anyway, because they get right to the point and are not filled with useless information.

If your eBook is short, tell people that it is a handy little guide to whatever your subject may be. They won't get any fluff or waffle – just the facts they will need to succeed in whatever you are writing about. Now that is a great benefit!

Let's look at a few other examples of things that could be thought of as negatives turned into positives:

- Negative – the eBook has no pictures.

- Positive – the eBook is packed with nothing but text and the type of information you want.

- Negative – the eBook only has three sections.

- Positive – the eBook contains everything you need in three easy to access sections.

- Negative – each chapter is only three or four pages long.

- Positive – each chapter contains just what you need to get ahead. No filler and no confusion. Exactly what you want!

Do you see how this works?

I'm sure you are probably thinking about your eBook in a brand new way now. You should be proud of your product—hey, you created it yourself—and now it's time to tell the world about just how good it is.

Tell people about the benefits of your eBook

Haven't we just covered this?

Not really. The positive aspects of your eBook aren't necessarily the same thing as benefits. Benefits go hand in hand with the features of your eBook, and it is important to make sure you understand the difference between them.

If that sounds a little confusing, don't worry. We'll go through this stage step by step to make sure it all falls into place for you.

I'm going to start with a little test for you. This test is probably the easiest way to get the difference between a benefit and a feature right from the start. So don't worry if you get this wrong, because it will still ensure you get it right—if that makes sense!

Which of the following two statements is a benefit and which one is a feature? Think about it before looking down the page to see the answer:

1. "This eBook also comes with two free videos on how to make money online within twenty four hours."

2. "This eBook comes with two free videos that will make sure you start earning money within twenty four hours of going online."

So did you get it right?

The first one was the feature, and the second one was the benefit. If you answered correctly, well done. In case you didn't, let's go back over the statements and see how this works.

If you read that first statement again, you will notice there is one very important thing missing from it:

"This eBook also comes with two free videos on how to make money online within twenty four hours."

The word 'you' is missing. This is incidentally a very good way of being able to tell whether you are giving people a feature or a benefit. If you have used the word 'you', then the chances are good that you have got a benefit.

The first statement tells us something about the eBook itself. Now that's wonderful, but it doesn't put the onus on the potential customer. You are telling them how great your eBook is, but you need to convince them that it has benefits for them, and that is exactly what the second statement does.

The best way to make sure you get this bit right is to make a list of all the features your eBook has. You can then go through that list and turn each one into a benefit.

Let's work through another example. Here are some features of a fictitious book:

- It has twenty pages.

- It comes with a free wall planner.

- It comes with a comprehensive list of resources.

Okay, now the first one is an easy one as we have already touched on this, so let's turn each one into a benefit for the potential buyer to think about:

- You will find this eBook easy to digest, as it only contains the facts that you need and nothing else.

- You will be able to stay on track and reach your goals with the free wall planner included.

- No more struggling to find the information you need; all you have to do is consult the list of resources included to know where to go next.

See how it works? I'm sure you can also see how to turn each one around, so a feature becomes a benefit. And of course, the word 'you' appears at least once in each and every example.

So remember—benefits over features.

The power of testimonials

What do you do before you buy a new product?

You might not do it all the time, but the chances are good that you will ask people you know if they have already tried it. And if they have, you will ask them what they thought of it. If the response is a good one, then you will be more likely to give it a go yourself.

Testimonials are wonderful because they really add strength to your sales page. Just imagine having a strong headline to introduce people to your product (more about that in just a moment...) and then launching into a testimonial so that people can see other people have already read your eBook and they love it.

Now I know what you are probably thinking. Your eBook isn't even published yet—and here we are talking about having some testimonials to put on your sales page.

How on earth are you going to get hold of those?

Well, think about all the people you know. Friends, family, extended family, people at work, and so on. Ask some of them if they would be willing to read your eBook and give you a written testimonial on what they thought. Make sure it is written because you can then copy and paste it into your web page. If they simply tell you, "Yeah, I thought it was great..." that's not much of a testimonial, is it?

You don't want to load your sales page with too many testimonials, but I've seen some pages with anything up to a dozen or thereabouts on them that have worked well, so bear that in mind. Incidentally, I have also seen websites that have had a few testimonials on them, and then they have given a link to a separate page on which there are dozens more, literally dozens.

This is a good tactic to use if your eBook is a success, and you receive lots of testimonials, and you want to use them all. It gives people the chance to read them if they wish, without cluttering up the whole sales page. If you use too many testimonials, it could end up being miles long, and people would lose interest in reading what the eBook itself was all about.

Another point to think about here is that you could include a request at the beginning of your eBook—on a separate page or perhaps as part of the preface—for people to send you their thoughts on the eBook. State that you may publish them on the sales page with their permission (always make sure you have their permission to do this).

You might also get ideas for future updates by doing this, as people will invariably ask about other aspects of the book or suggest things for future editions.

Once you start getting testimonials from customers, you can add them to the ones you already have or replace them if you wish.

There is no doubt, however, that testimonials are an excellent way to improve your sales page. In fact, if you search online for any kind of eBook on any subject under the sun, you will be hard pushed to find one that doesn't have any testimonials on it at all.

The unique selling point

Your unique selling point is also known as USP. This is what makes your eBook stand out from all the other ones that are written about the same subject. Look through your eBook while asking this question—what makes your eBook on weight loss unique and different?

- Does it have case studies from real people who have used the methods described to lose weight?

148

- Do you give people a step by step "roadmap" to follow so that they will know the steps involved in this way of eating?

- Is there a list of forbidden foods?

- Are there menus or lists of food combinations that work well?

- Have you come up with a new, safe technique for weight loss that is so simple, anyone can follow it?

- Do you offer a money back guarantee if people fail to lose weight within a certain period of time?

The headline

The headline is what will grab people's attention when they reach your mini-site sales page. It is the eBook's equivalent of a drumroll. So it needs to be big!

It has to tell the truth with no bull—and be something that people will believe. Don't forget that. We're trying to get a balance between telling the truth and encouraging a feeling of excitement and trepidation in the reader.

It needs to tell them what to do when they reach the end of this sales page and how to order the product. Remember, your main headline has about four seconds to spark the reader's curiosity enough to make them continue investigating the offer.

Here are some examples of the kind of thing you will often see online:

- "This $15,000/week secret saved me from my burger flipping career..."

- "Now you can do what I'm doing to earn an extra $3,000 a week with little effort..."

- "Who else would like to discover the secret of shedding those excess pounds and finally achieving the weight they dream of?"

There is usually a little teaser above the headline which helps to lead you into the web page itself, but the teaser isn't essential and indeed it often gets overlooked by the headline. You see, the teaser (something like 'I'm still pinching myself, but I've discovered something amazing...' or something similar) is almost like the pause before the drum roll. Not everyone will notice it; it helps if they do, but even if they don't, they'll hear that drum roll for sure.

The headline appears in much larger color type, not black, that is usually red. It's going to be the first thing that will catch the eye of every single person who lands on your sales page. This is the first thing that the reader will see and you have about four seconds to pull them further into your sales page. The longer you keep the reader on the page the better the chance of making the sale.

Some people find that writing the all important headline is much worse than writing the whole eBook! The main headline is where you have 80% opportunity to make the sale. Here are some pointers as to what a great headline will have in it:

- Benefit
- Guarantee/Promise
- Suspense
- Intrigue
- Curiosity

A benefit followed by a guarantee is a common equation. For example, "Lose 50 pounds in 2 months". "Lose 50 pounds" is the benefit and "in 2 months" is the guarantee or promise. Now you just need to jazz it up with suspense, intrigue, and or curiosity, such as "Lose 50 pounds in 2 months and reduce your electric bill". Exercise bicycle connected to a generator to feed electricity to a battery bank that offsets your peak electric demands... Ok, lame, but do you get the idea? Lack of patience can result in headlines that can be improved, which is why the next section is important.

Take a good look at it. Does it do what you want it to do? Does it convey a passion and desire to want to know more? Try to find some other ways of saying the same thing—it could be that you are on the right track, but you just need to strengthen the way you say it a little more. In most cases the headline can be shortened—the shorter the better. It is amazing how many words you can cut out of a headline if you really focus on cutting it to the bone without changing the meaning. You can always do some work on the headline and then leave it while you edit the rest of the page. Then go back to it again to see if you still feel the same about it.

Drama and suspense

Drama and suspense are what keep you watching and waiting through the ad break while you are waiting for the next part of your favorite program to come on. They are what keep you biting your nails all week while you're waiting to see what happens in episode two of that new show.

What you need to do is to tell people about your product without revealing too much of the actual content. One technique that works really well is by revealing a little of what is on certain pages:

- "Page 2 reveals how to make $100 in your first week online...""Discover how to save more money this month than you did the whole of last year on page 17..."

- "Don't think you can feed a family of four on just two dollars? Be proven wrong on page 35..."

I'm sure you'll agree that all these examples are intriguing and would make anyone want to click on that order button!

You can see how they are telling people a little about what is in the actual eBook they will be getting... without actually telling them much at all. They know that on page 2 they will find out about a method for making a hundred dollars during their first week online. That's a great promise because they will be thinking, "Hey, if I order this now I could be a hundred dollars better off by this time next week!"

See how they are already thinking positively about buying your eBook?

In that second example, they will be thinking about how much money they made last year. Let's say they made $25,000. So now they'll be sitting there thinking, "Hey, just imagine how my life could change if I could earn twenty five grand a month?!"

And in that third example, people on a budget with a family to feed will certainly be thinking about how much easier their budgeting could be if they were able to feed them all on just two dollars. They could even start saving a little cash here and there if that were really possible.

They readers are given the hook, and they take it and keep reading. They want to know what else this eBook can do for them. And if you give them enough good reasons, they will certainly go all out and buy it from you.

But there's another great method for ensuring that people keep reading, and I have been using it from time to time in this very book that you're reading now. It involves telling people that something good is coming up... but not revealing it straightaway.

For example, I know that the issue of pricing has probably gone through your head already. I also know that there is a chapter coming up soon in this book which deals with the ins and outs of that very subject.

So what I could do is write something like this:

"Of course, you have the option of giving your eBook away for free. You might think that sounds crazy—after all, you've spent all this time and energy and hard work creating a superb product. Why on earth would you want to give it away for nothing? Well, I will reveal the reason why you would do just that very shortly. But first..."

You see what I mean? I've told you that something really good is coming up, but I haven't told you exactly what. I have effectively sign-

152

posted it so you know what to expect, but the secret hasn't yet been completely revealed.

Oh, and by the way, that example is completely true. I am going to tell you why you might want to give your eBook away free of charge, and it's coming up in a later chapter. Aren't you just itching to find out more?

When should you reveal the price?

The price is never revealed until the very end of the page, and is usually followed by a money back guarantee. Make sure you include one of these because you will actually get more sales if you do—people won't risk buying something if they know they won't get their money back if they don't like it. And if your eBook is good that shouldn't happen too often anyway.

It's important to reiterate the benefits of your eBook once you have told them the price of it as well. Once they see the amount of money they will have to pay to get hold of your eBook, they might start finding reasons why they shouldn't buy it. So it's up to you to give them reasons why they should.

Call to action

Now this might sound crazy, but you need to tell people what they have to do when they are on your sales page. It's obvious that you want them to buy the eBook, but you need to give them a little more direction than that. This direction is a call to action.

For example, instead of just saying "Buy my eBook now!" and then leaving them to figure out where the order button is, make things as easy as you possibly can for them.

Say something like this instead—"All you need to do to get your copy of my eBook right now is to click on the order button below. That will take you into my secure payment processor, and once you've paid for your purchase, you can start reading my eBook right away!"

Do you see how this tells people exactly how to do it, in a step by step fashion? Some people think this equates to talking down to people, and it does in a way, but if you do it carefully, you can get it right. If you give them an exact set of instructions, then you won't have to worry about whether or not everyone will be able to figure out how they order.

You will also notice that the above example gives out those step by step instructions in a positive and exciting way. It makes a point of revealing that it will only take a few moments to place the order, pay for it, and then receive the eBook. That gets across another benefit of ordering eBooks online, and it may sway a few people who aren't sure whether to order it or not.

Make sure you mention your secure payment processor as well. You can set up the secure payment processor via PayPal if you wish; which makes it easy to put order buttons on your mini-site, and PayPal takes care of all the security issues as well. If you can offer good security, then less people will be worrying about whether they can use their credit card to pay you or not. If you use ClickBank you won't need PayPal to process payments.

You can also make sure they get into the habit of thinking that they will buy your eBook, simply by telling them that in your sales pitch. Take a look at the following two sentences and consider the difference between them:

- "If you decide to buy my eBook, you will find that chapter three contains some very revealing information on how I made $2,000 in a single day..."

- "When you read my eBook, you will no doubt want to discover the secret in chapter three on how I made $2,000 in a single day and you can too."

Do you see the subtle difference? The first example contains the word 'if'. This word is a no no in sales letters—at least as far as the actual idea of people buying your eBook is concerned. Don't put any doubt in their minds at all; you won't be able to convince everyone who reads your sales page to buy your eBook, but you don't want to turn anyone away by making them feel indecisive either.

The second example assumes that people are going to read your eBook, which assumes that people are going to buy it too. You're also speaking to the reader in a more direct way, mentioning the word 'you' four times and the word 'your' once. In contrast, the first example only contains the word 'you' once; the onus is more on you as the writer and what you achieved—not what the reader could achieve.

It's all a question of making sure that your readers think they are going to get your eBook—even before they have made that decision.

PS - Don't forget the PS!

Guess which section of your sales page is the second most read? Yes, the PS. A large percentage of the readers will be intrigued by the main headline, skim the body while looking for the price, and read the PS. Many copy writers lose focus or get burned out by the time they get to the PS. Don't let this happen to you. Focus on this almost as much as the main headline and use several PSs (PS, PPS, PPPS, etc). Highlight all the benefits to convince readers that their world will stop spinning if they don't purchase your product right this moment.

What they will see when they reach the end of the page are the main advantages that exist in buying your product. Here are some of the main ones you might see:

- A 60-day no questions asked money back guarantee (as per ClickBank requirements).

- A list of phenomenal bonuses that add value to the core product.

- A reminder of the amazing benefits and how the eBook will change the reader's life.

The idea is two fold here—if you get someone who reads your headline and then shoots to the bottom of the page, they will see the best arguments for buying your eBook. And if they read through the entire page from start to finish as you intend them to, they will simply be reminded of those points once they have finished.

In this sense the power of the PS comes in two versions, and it makes it an essential component on any sales page.

We've looked at every part of writing the sales copy for your mini-site sales page. It helps if you read through each bit more than once, so that you get the hang of how it will work. Crafting sales copy is a science and art that can take decades of focused experience to excel in this discipline. If you wish to learn from a master copywriter you can purchase Dan Kennedy's 'The Ultimate Sales Letter: Attract New Customers. Boost Your Sales' (ISBN 978-1593374990).

We're going to move forward and make sure that your sales page stands the best possible chance of being found on the search engines.

Optimizing your sales page for search engines

Don't assume that you will be listed on the search engines from the moment you launch your mini-site. It could take some weeks for it to happen, and a lot can depend on how much traffic you start getting from other sources.

To get your mini-site found quickly and indexed quickly by the search engines you should follow the strategies in Chapter 14.

But back to optimization—search engine optimization or SEO as it's commonly called.

What you need to do is to make sure you include a variety of different keywords and phrases in your copy that people interested in the topic of your eBook are likely to search for.

How do you know which ones to use?

Well, you go through the same process you went through when you were researching topics to write an eBook about in the first place. Only this time you are looking at the results you get back as a whole. Use more than one keyword tool for this—you want to get a broad view of the different phrases people are using to find information that will be included in your eBook.

When you do this exercise, you usually end up with a handful of words and phrases you will want to use more than others. Certain phrases may only be searched for quite rarely, but you may still want to pop them in once or twice if you can.

Incorporating keywords into sales page

This is the challenging bit! I'm sure you've read sales pages where the author has obviously put the need for keyword density above the need for a well written page.

Make sure your writing comes first, even if that means missing out on a few keywords. You are the person who has written the eBook, and if your sales page isn't that good, you can bet the people reading it won't want to read the eBook itself.

Keyword density, by the way, is the term given to the percentage of keywords in any given piece of text. While there is no definitive figure that you should aim for in this respect, most people will advise against going above five per cent for any one keyword/phrase, and less is safer.

All you need to do is to work out how many keywords are in your sales page, and divide it by the total number of words in the page. Then you multiply it by one hundred to get the total percentage of keywords. That's your keyword density.

You'll know when you get too many keywords in there because the page won't read naturally. If you look at what you have written and all you can see are the various keywords staring back at you, you've probably put too many in!

As the sales page reads naturally and tells the reader everything they want to know, you'll be fine. In actual fact it is quite difficult to write a comprehensive sales page about your eBook and not include lots of relevant keywords.

Editing your sales page

We're back to editing again I'm afraid. Many of the editing techniques we discussed before will apply here too, so there's no need to go over them again.

The only thing I would say is that your sales page needs to be exciting and vibrant. Really sell your eBook—don't just tell people about it in a shy way and hope they will buy. You need to do the best you can here.

So do the same thing you did with your eBook and put your first draft of the sales page away before you edit it. When you come back and read it again with fresh eyes, ask yourself if you feel motivated enough to buy it.

You'll know the answer—and you'll then know how much editing you have to do.

Conclusion

This has been a big chapter, and for good reason. I'm sure you can see how important your mini-site is when you have an eBook to sell.

Don't be afraid to spend a lot of time on this. You're better off to do that than you are to rush out a half hearted version that won't get traffic or attract much interest.

Just before you launch your mini-site, when everything is complete and you are ready to go, take one last look at the sale page. Is it the best you can do? Have you labored over every detail?

If you have and you are happy, then it's time to start making sales. It's also time to think about selling your eBook in some other great places as well, and that's what we're going to look at next.

Chapter 11:
Selling Your EBook on ClickBank

Your mini-site is launched. Well done! That's a big step for anyone to take.

Let's take things a step further now, starting with a question. How would you like to have an army of people promoting your eBook for you? And would you like them to do it for free unless they sold a copy? Well, it's not a pipe dream, it's a reality, and it comes to you courtesy of the mini-site www.clickbank.com.

ClickBank has given many eBook writers the chance to vastly increase their sales with over 100,000 affiliates looking for quality products to promote.

So what is ClickBank?

ClickBank is a website that brings authors and affiliates together. Authors can join the website in the hope that affiliate members may want to promote and earn from their eBook.

But for affiliates (for whom registration is free) there is an opportunity to make a big income by promoting authors' eBooks. ClickBank manages the sales tracking, affiliate revenue, affiliate and author payouts, and payment processing, which provides a hands-off solution.

ClickBank's services are well worth the small fee that authors will pay to take advantage of this opportunity to dramatically increase their sales. The website is also well thought out and there is a good help section. A great resource for learning the tips, tricks, and strategies of ClickBank is to join Harvey Segal and Adrian Ling's forum at www.clickbanksuccessforum.com.

There are plenty of FAQ sections and resources for both affiliates and sellers on the website, and that makes it very useful to both. This is one of the top websites that brings affiliates and publishers together.

Are you getting curious? Let's find out a little about how it all works.

The process of selling on ClickBank

A great thing about ClickBank is that you only pay the signup fee once. Currently set at $49.95, and is promoted as an activation fee to open your account.

But you don't even need to pay that until you have gone through the process of getting that first eBook set up. There are a number of steps that need to be followed properly, and it is highly advisable to read through all the terms, conditions and frequently asked questions (FAQs) that the website offers.

Not only will this ensure you understand everything before you sign up, but it will prevent delays in getting your eBook online and visible to affiliates. For example, if you were planning on writing an eBook about making money by promoting it through social networking websites, you'll have to forget about ClickBank as they don't allow them. In reality there are very few exceptions, and most of them are obvious when you think about it.

You will need to submit your eBook to ClickBank and wait for approval before it goes live where affiliates can view your information. If your eBook is about an inappropriate topic, is poor quality, or if you broke a one of the rules, you'll be able to make changes and resubmit.

On the ClickBank website, they state that you need a pitch page. That's simply another term for a sales page, so we've covered that already. Just make sure it meets all their requirements.

You should note that if you are going to use ClickBank, your payment link will go through their website. This is so they can monitor who sends the customers to your mini-site, and who makes the sales for you.

ClickBank has a few requirements your mini-site must follow, so make sure they are all included. They are all quite simple though, such as the need to make it crystal clear how much the customer has to pay to receive your product. Be sure you check the ClickBank website to see exactly what is required.

You should be able to write your sales page and then tweak it if necessary though; there's nothing much to worry about there.

Make sure you promote the fact that people can sell your eBook and receive a commission. If you have a blog, you'll certainly be mentioning that you are going to launch your latest (or first) eBook on ClickBank. So why not mention that to your readers so they can sell it too?

Once you have set up your product with ClickBank and received product approval you should create another account that you will use for your own affiliate links. The first thing you want to do is use your affiliate account to create an affiliate link (hoplink) to your eBook sales page. Click on your affiliate link and purchase your own eBook. This is the same as someone else buying your eBook, but when you do it immediately after product approval your eBook will be listed in the ClickBank Market Place and it will have a gravity of 1. There isn't enough space to cover all the great tips about how to sell successfully through ClickBank, so consider downloading the free ClickBank for Newbies guide at http://www.clickbankguide.com/clickbank-newbies.htm from ClickBank Guru Harvey Segal.

And don't forget that in chapter fourteen, we'll be exploring lots of ways to promote your eBook. Why not promote the affiliate opportunity as well? All you need to do is send them to ClickBank to sign up for free, and they can get started right away.

ClickBank benefits and drawbacks

As with most websites, there are good points and bad points to selling on ClickBank. Many authors have made a lot of money by having their product(s) listed on the website, but others haven't succeeded at all.

This is not meant to scare or disappoint you, but you should be aware of the situation so that you can decide whether it's right for you or not. For example, some of the best selling products on ClickBank are related to making money online. This doesn't mean that your product has to be on that same subject; it just means that you know products in that category tend to do well.

A lot will obviously depend on how good your eBook and sales page really are. Affiliates will be able to see your sales page before they decide whether or not to promote your product. This means that the better your sales page is, the more chance you have of convincing more people to promote it for you.

Be patient. You may not get a flood of people promoting your eBook from the second it appears on ClickBank. Being realistic will help—it could take time to get that first sale. It also depends on how active you are in telling potential affiliates about the opportunity they have to promote your eBook for you.

The more promoting you do, the more affiliates you are going to have promoting the eBook for you.

One of the main benefits is that ClickBank will handle the provision of a secure server to take payments over. They will also pay you your earnings each week through direct deposit or twice monthly with a check. Once everything is set up you should focus your attention on attracting affiliates to promote your eBook.

Another possible drawback could be that there are already thousands of eBooks on ClickBank. That could be construed as a good thing, since the website is clearly a popular and successful way to generate more sales of a good eBook.

It also means there is a lot of competition. This competition means you need to use every facility the website gives you to make sure your eBook will be found and promoted by its users. Part of that is writing a great eBook with a tempting title that really delivers on its promises and the other part of it is to write a terrific sales page.

Make sure your product will be found when people use the Click-Bank search engine in the marketplace as well. Making sure your product will be found is a simple process, and it simply means that you need to choose the most relevant category for your product to go into. Choosing the relevant category for your product will happen once your product has been approved for sale. You'll find what you need under 'My Site' on your personal account screen.

Most affiliates will search for products to promote by using the marketplace search facility, so it makes perfect sense to ensure your product can be found there.

Perhaps the biggest benefit of ClickBank is the scope you have to make more sales. While it is obviously true that some books do better than others, having access to thousands of affiliates is very powerful. Even if only a handful of people are going to promote your book, you could make sales you would never have made otherwise.

So in short, the advantages of ClickBank far outweigh any disadvantages. And since you can promote up to five hundred products for that single activation charge, I think you'd better get writing!

In fact, this can be a good way of deciding on your next eBook project. Why not find out what the most popular products are on ClickBank in a particular category and think along those lines for writing your next book? Don't copy what has already been done, but see if there is a gap there that you could fill. Just remember to do your keyword research and usual bout of homework before you start writing.

How much commission should you offer affiliates?

You'll invariably do better if you offer a better rate of commission on sold copies of your eBook as well. If there were two eBooks that covered the same subject, but one offered double the amount of commission the other one was offering, which one would you go for if you were an affiliate? It's a no brainer, isn't it?

Skimping on your commission rates will only result in getting fewer sales. Most of the top selling publishers offer 75% of each sale to the affiliate.

You may not be comfortable paying affiliates higher commissions than you receive, but you haven't had to promote your eBook at all to get that sale. The affiliates have done the hard work, so they should be rewarded as such.

Try to provide a quality product so that you can charge as much as possible and offer the maximum of 75% commission to affiliates. You will attract many more affiliates, and possibly super affiliates if your affiliate profit per sale is attractive, such as over $30 per sale. Super affiliates with emails lists of hundreds of thousands can put a ton of cash in your pocket with a single email blast, and they aren't interested in small commissions. Affiliates with large email lists typically won't promote a product unless the profit per sale is $50 and up.

Try increasing the value of your product offering by adding a second eBook, special report, how-to videos, *etc.* This will get more qualified affiliates on board, and customers will appreciate value-added products.

It is up to you though. Check out the pricing of the more successful eBooks to become familiar with pricing strategies and price points.

Conclusion

That was a brief look at the benefits of ClickBank. But there are also other places to sell your eBook online, and we're going to look at another big venue in the very next chapter.

Stay tuned though, because a little later in this eBook I'll be sharing some other possibilities with you too. Are you starting to see just how much potential this business has? I know it seems like a lot of information, but if you take it step-by-step you can make it through the process and each new eBook becomes easier and faster to get to market.

Chapter 12:
Selling Your EBook on Amazon

Can you imagine how cool it would be to sell your eBook on the biggest book selling site on the internet?

Amazon is the biggest book selling website, and you can sell your eBook alongside the publishing greats, if you do it properly. And that's what you will learn in this chapter.

Why sell on Amazon?

Amazon is huge. If you want a book and you're going to buy it online, chances are Amazon is the first place you think of.

Many self published authors found their eBook sales increased incredibly just by adding their book to Amazon. The number of copies you can sell can be very high.

Amazon opens the biggest internet book buying audience for authors and publishers where buyers can find your eBook by typing keywords into the Amazon search tool.

Selling your eBook on Amazon for Kindle Reader

Amazon now offers digital downloads to its Kindle wireless reading device. Kindle is a book sized electronic eBook reader that Amazon developed so that it only has to deal with one eBook format, while also making money from the Kindle reader sales. It differs wildly from print on demand (POD) publishing, which we will be looking at in chapter fifteen. Digital fulfillment basically refers to an eBook that is sent wirelessly to the customer's Kindle reader as a digital file. There are a few requirements for selling electronic documents using this service, which include:

- You must be a US citizen.

- You must have and provide to Amazon your social insurance number.

- You must have a bank account.

Unless you meet all three conditions above you cannot sell on Amazon.

Amazon provides you with 35% of the list price of each eBook sold. Amazon keeps the rest. This may seems like a small percentage, especially if Amazon doesn't have to print or ship any books, but that is the way it is. It is no different than paying an affiliate commission of 65%, though it is difficult to sell your eBooks on Kindle for the same prices as those sold using mini-sites. An interesting thing with Amazon is that you can put your eBook on sale at a lower price and still receive the same 35% commission of the list price.

You also need to submit your eBook in HTML format, not PDF. Using your word processor (Word, WordPerfect, or Open Office) with your eBook file open, click on File, then Save As, and select HTML as the file type.

Sign up for an account at www.digitaltextplatform.com by simply adding your personal information, author name, book title, and price. Then upload your file and in 24-48 hours you will be selling on Amazon.

Chapter 13:
How to Price Your EBook

You've done all your research, and you sat down and accomplished what a lot of people simply cannot manage to do, and that's write the darn eBook in the first place. And what's more, you've also persevered and managed to keep going and built a good mini-site and sales page to prepare for product launch.

There's only one thing missing now. And that's the price. Let's take a look at what could happen if you went too far in either direction.

Pricing your eBook too high

This has several disadvantages, both with copies that you do sell and copies that you don't. Let me explain.

Let's say you find a mini-site that is promoting a brand new eBook. And let's say you really like the look of this eBook. You want to buy it. You want to learn from it and use the information inside it to make your life better in some way.

By the time you get to the bottom of the sales page, where the price becomes apparent, you are sold on the eBook. You've practically got your credit card out and you're looking for the pay now button.

And then you see the price.

And unfortunately there is no way you can afford it. As much as you want to get the eBook, the price is probably double what you could justify paying. So you have to pass it up.

This scenario happens often because some authors are intent on getting the most money they can for their product. Now it's fair enough that you want to make a nice chunk of change for your efforts, but if you price it out of the market you are aiming at, it won't sell.

Think of it like this. Would you consider taking a Porsche into a run down part of town to try and sell it? Of course not, because the product doesn't match the market. But you'd probably sell a less expensive car without any problem.

When you are thinking about setting the price, think about two things:

- What you are offering?
- Who you are offering it to?

Those are the two main points you need to think about with each eBook you write.

If you have written a comprehensive eBook about making money online, you'll need to think about who it is aimed at. If you have aimed it at people who have already had some success, you could probably charge more for it than you would if you were aiming at people who wanted to get started on a shoestring budget. If they don't have the money to invest in getting started on a large scale, they won't have a large sum of money to invest in your eBook either.

Pricing your eBook too low

Your eBook can actually sell fewer copies if you price it too low. It sounds amazing, but if you have ever had a browse around eBay or any other auction site online where you don't see the goods before you buy them, what is your reaction if you see something selling for a very low price?

The perception is often that the product is cheap and of poor quality, and that perception is there for eBooks as well.

So how much do you charge?

There are two beliefs I want to share with you here:

- I firmly believe that every eBook has its ideal, perfect price.
- I also firmly believe that in most instances you will need to experiment to find out what it is.

Determine a starting price by taking a look at what other people are charging for similar books on ClickBank and on Amazon.

You also need to be honest with yourself about the quality and value of the content you are providing. If you followed the steps I shared with you in this book, you will probably have written something that is unique and provides valuable content.

Always, always, always, make sure you start at the highest price you think the market will pay. If you start it low and then try and put the price up later on, you'll lose loads of people who might otherwise have bought it. And with ClickBank, once your product and price are approved you can lower the price, but if you want to increase the price you need to submit to ClickBank for approval again. If you start high and lower the price, you will attract attention, not divert it.

The exception to this rule is known as something of a marketing gimmick that big eBook sellers often use. This occurs when they set their price lower than they intend to, with the caveat that it will go up at some point in the near future to another specified price, or they have a one time offer (OTO) that they will increase the profits of the transaction. Another strategy is using the low ball price to collect email addresses for future product sales using email marketing.

But you can never be sure what your optimum price will be. I read a story recently where the author revealed that he had tried selling his eBook at several different prices. We'll call them high, medium and low—the actual amounts don't really matter.

What he found was that the low price attracted too few orders because people thought it was too cheap. There has to be some catch, surely, they must have been thinking. Remember what we found out above?

The high price was simply too high, so in the end he settled for somewhere in the middle. And in fact that was the price that buyers paid most readily. It was obviously high enough to give the impression that the book had value, without being too far out of that market's price range.

Have you ever noticed that many products on ClickBank and other venues sell for a price ending in 7 and 9? In the marketing world it is a known fact that products ending in 7 and 9 outsell other prices. So price your book at $47, or $37.97, or 97, etc.

So be prepared to experiment to see what works best for you. And don't be afraid to try a higher price initially because it could be just what the market will bear.

Come and get my free eBook!

Now hang on a minute, isn't the whole purpose of this eBook about wanting to make money from writing eBooks of your own?

Yes it is, and nothing has changed in that respect. But as ironic as it sounds it can actually work in your favor to start distributing an eBook that you have written for free.

If you write an eBook and give it away for free, it has the ability to 'go viral'. That might sound like a nasty disease, but in actual fact you want this to happen if at all possible.

What many eBook writers do is write a free version of another, larger eBook that they have written. Your free eBook can be anything from a dozen pages to something much longer, but it's important to remember that if you are using it as a pre-cursor to your main eBook, it shouldn't just be a long sales letter. It should give real value and anyone who reads it should come away from it knowing things they didn't know before. In short, it should be useful and usable even if they decide not to go ahead and buy the big version.

For example, let's say you write an eBook that covers various ways of making a living working from home. You could then write a free eBook with an intriguing title that is based on the same area of interest. How about, "Are you the right person to work successfully from home?", for example. You want your free eBook to attract the right people who would also be very likely to buy your main eBook, and if you include your mini-site address at the foot of every page of your freebie as we mentioned earlier, you've got plenty of opportunities for each reader to click through and visit your mini-site.

There is something else you should do as well when it comes to writing a free eBook for distribution in this way. After your title page, make sure you have a page which basically lists you as the writer and holder of the copyright. Below this, add a message which says something like this:

"You are welcome to distribute this eBook in any way you wish, either as a bonus or a freebie, but you may not charge anyone for the privilege."

By stating clearly that people can pass it on to others you are increasing the chances that they will do just that. And when you think that every person who receives it could pass it on to still more people, you can see why some of these eBooks do go viral and spread very quickly throughout the internet.

Your free eBook could also be used to build your mailing list. Offer the freebie in exchange for a person's name and email address, and you can then send them details of your other books when they become available.

There is also the question of building trust. People are far more likely to download a free eBook than they are to pay for it, if they haven't heard of you before. If they don't know who you are, you've got no track record in their eyes so they won't know how efficient or worthwhile your book might be.

Now if they read your freebie and they like what you have to say, what do you think the chances are of them buying your next eBook if it is on a similar subject? I'd say the chances are much higher.

So think about whether you could create a free eBook to help boost your business further. In the long run, a free copy can increase your income and your reputation even more.

Bonuses

To increase sales you can 'sweetening the deal'. This is the eBook equivalent of the food store's 'buy one get one free', or 'buy this printer and get the ink cartridges free'. The point is that you are giving the customer a better deal by offering freebies with your main eBook.

So what's the best freebie to offer?

The main rule is that any freebie should be related to your main product. It's no good offering something completely unrelated, even if it is a great product, because people will be interested in the subject of your eBook, not anything else. The more related and the more the perceived value, the more likely it is that you will get the sale.

You could offer a couple of free reports with useful information going into more depth on aspects related to your main eBook. For an eBook on saving money on your groceries, you could include a report revealing the top sources of money saving information on this topic on the internet. Anything practical, quick to write, and easy to read and digest and with a persuasive title will work well.

Anyone interested in saving money on their food shopping is very likely to want to save money in other areas too, such as how to reduce your electric bill and how to save money on car repairs.

You need at least two high quality bonuses and preferably more. Some publishers offer so many bonuses to beef up their sales page that it would be half the length it actually is if they got rid of all the bonuses!

Should you use your own bonuses—or PLR?

You can also search around online to see if you can find any related eBooks that you can give away for free or pay a one-time fee to join a private label rights (PLR) membership website. A quick search on the internet will provide you with hundreds of PLR websites to choose from.

There is nothing wrong with doing this, and indeed if you want to get your new eBook up and running and on sale as quickly as possible it can save you time. Many of the biggest eBook sellers will offer bonuses created by other people.

The main thing to remember is that you must double check that you have the rights to give them away for free AND you can re-brand the product with your own links (to your products that you are selling). Often you can also modify graphics, logo, modify text, etc., but the most important thing is to insert links in the free product so the reader can click on them and potentially purchase your other products. If your bonuses are unique, the perceived value is higher. One thing to watch for is that many PLR products are on the low quality side which may be because the writing was outsourced overseas to low wage writers with English as their second or third language.

If you have the time and the resources, you should give away your own bonuses, purely because they are directly related to your book and you are in complete control of the quality. Bonuses you might provide to your readers include:

- A two-page action plan for the next two months showing what needs to be done each day to write an eBook, as an example. The main product itself will be the nuts and bolts how-to information.

- A how-to video tutorial.

- A software program that will make using your main product, or the customers' main goal, easier to complete.

- A special report on a related subject.

You now have your eBook, bonuses, and it's all packaged up and looking good. All you need to do now is sell it!

Chapter 14:
Promoting Your EBook

Promotion is vital if you want to cash in on your effort. Some people think that it's enough to write a great sales page, buy that domain name, and set up a mini-site to sell the eBook from. But that is just the start.

There are many ways to promote your eBook, including free and low cost options. Let's take a look at some of the methods you can use to get more traffic to your mini-site.

Press releases

Press releases are announcements which tell people about a newsworthy event that is about to happen. Alternatively, they can announce something that has just taken place or an eBook that has been released.

The number one rule for writing a press release is contained in that paragraph above. You need something newsworthy to tell the world about. And what better news could there be than an announcement of the fact that you have released your first (or latest) eBook?

The good news is that there are several companies online that will distribute your press release for free. A good example is www.prlog.org and there are plenty more that you will find on any search engine. You'll find details of www.prlog.org and others in the resources section at the back of this book.

Many websites have tips and advice on how to write a good press release that gets attention, but there are two tips in particular that are worth mentioning here. First, and it is worth repeating, you need to have a newsworthy event to write about. Launching a new eBook certainly qualifies, but if you want to write a press release about an eBook you published some time ago, you'll need to find a new angle. An option for an older eBook is to update it with fresh information. We spoke about this earlier, and it is certainly a big enough event to write about.

If you launch your eBook and you experience good sales, then you could use that as the basis for a press release. For example, your first release would be along the lines of 'Brand new eBook is released', while your second one would have a title more like 'New eBook on [subject of eBook or title] sells x number of copies in the first hour'. Or day, or week or whatever applies. Be creative with your press releases, and you can get more publicity than you might think.

Just be sure each press release is original since search engines prefer new and original content. You can check your work for uniqueness at www.copyscape.com. This will lead to better results in the results of search engines. And remember those keywords! It certainly won't harm you to pop a few of those in the release either, especially in the title and two or three in the press release body.

The second point is to make sure you state the facts and don't write to anyone in particular. This requires an altogether different writing style from the one you used to write your eBook. Imagine going from talking to one person to simply announcing an event without talking to anyone at all! It does feel strange, but it's fairly easy to pick up, and there is a way that you can ensure you get it right every time.

A good way of making sure you don't write to anyone in particular is to check your release after you have written it. What you need to do is strike out every occasion where you have used the word 'you'.

Here's an example:

- BAD – "You can find cheaper insurance using the info in this eBook."
- GOOD – "Everyone can find cheaper insurance using the info in this eBook."

It's a subtle difference, but a big one. If a company that distributes press releases receives one which is full of sentences like the ones in the first example, you will very likely receive it back. You can edit it and resubmit of course, but why not get things right first time?

It's also important to make sure that you lay your press release out properly. You should have your contact details at the top of the release, aligned to the right hand side of the page. Following that, make

176

sure you center the words 'For immediate release' and add the month and the year too.

Your headline is next. Make sure it states the facts and makes it clear exactly what the newsworthy event actually is. Once you've done all that, you should write around 500 words for the release itself. This length should allow plenty of room to include the details.

Free press release distribution websites will have guidelines on submission requirements, and it is worth the time to read through the guidelines to ensure that you adhere to their exact requirements.

Tip - quotations in press releases hold the readers' interest and make your press release more readable. This might seem strange when you are writing about the eBook that you have written! But all you need to do is to come up with some quotations from you that are relevant to your eBook.

If you get stuck, here are some sample questions for you. Use the answers you come up with to give you some ideas for quotations:

- What made you write this eBook?

- Have you had personal experience of what you are writing about?

- How do you think other people will benefit from it?

- What feedback have you had already?

- Has it already proved successful?

- Why have you added new updated information to it?

These questions should be enough to get you started. And again, the best advice if you are stuck is to go online and read some of the press releases that have already been published (see www.prlog.org).

Think about when you will need to issue a press release and think about as many newsworthy events that you can in the life of your eBook. The more events there are, the more publicity you will be able to get as a result.

Include contact details on your press release. These should either be for you personally or if you are part of a larger company, the person who is in the best position to field questions and queries about the subject of the release. If you don't include any contact details, there is again a very high chance that your release won't be published.

There are three things you absolutely must have in place if you are to rise above the thousands of other press releases out there and stand a chance of being published and seen by the very people you are trying to reach.

Writing a good press release

Every good press release follows a template, and while this varies from source to source the template I have included in this section will certainly do the job.

You'll notice that I have included a sub-heading in this template; this is because a lot of press releases use them to alert readers to an additional fact about the event that is particularly important.

Here are some examples which show you how a sub-heading can be used to your advantage:

- "New widget is the least expensive available"
- "200th addition to Widget World's range"
- "Widget World Opening Day on April 15th 2008"

You can see how your sub-heading allows you to share another snippet of useful information about your newsworthy event, so it should be used wisely.

Here is the template itself:

Your name

Contact details (inc. phone number)

FOR IMMEDIATE RELEASE

PRESS RELEASE HEADLINE

Sub heading if needed

Body of release

For more information—contact details need to go here, along with a website address to visit if relevant.

You'll see that there isn't really any big secret to this; it's simply a case of organizing your material properly and making sure you include all the necessary information in the right places.

Many people find that when it comes to writing their release it is easier to jot down the facts before they start. This makes the writing much easier to do, because you know exactly what you have to say. Press releases are usually 500 words long and rarely spill onto a second page (although they may do if there are plenty of paragraphs in the body of the release itself, which make it easier to read). Your notes will therefore make it much easier to write an effective release.

Quote, unquote

If you really want to transform your press release from something that does the job into something that really catches the eye, use the power of quotations to get you there.

We're always interested in what people have to say, and even if you are listed as the contact on your release and you are the person who is writing it, you can still include your own quotes as part of the release in order to strengthen it and enable it to catch the eye even more than it already has.

Just imagine the kind of questions people might ask you about the subject of your release. Let's take another look at that widget example from earlier. If someone asked you why you invented a customizable widget what would you say? And what if someone asked you why you didn't invent it sooner what would be your reply?

Good quotations break up the main portion of the release by providing added interest in between the factual paragraphs. They also enable you to get more information across to the reader in a more interesting way, which makes it more likely that they will read the entire release instead of just the beginning.

Good search engine optimization (SEO) techniques also apply to press releases. If you are using the press release to direct people to your mini-site, you should use the same keywords throughout the press release in the order of preference as listed in the keyword meta tags on the webpage you are pointing to. If you don't know what a meta tag is don't worry, just provide your website designer with a list of your keywords in order of highest priority (primary keyword) to lowest. Make certain to include your primary keyword in the title page and resource section. Be certain not to exceed 2% keyword density for your primary keyword or keyphrase as it may get rejected for spamming. Sprinkle the remaining keywords throughout the press release. You can check the keyword density of your web pages and your press release (if you upload it to test it) using the tool at www.seochat.com.

If you are using Microsoft Word to write your press release, you may want to save the document as a Plain Text document as required by certain press release services.

Submitting your release for publication

There are several ways you can do this, but by far the easiest is to submit it to online press release services – some of which will distribute it free of charge.

You will generally find that the free services offer a limited distribution service, while if you pay for your release to be circulated you will have the potential to reach a far bigger audience. I would recommend that you start off with the free services and only use the paid ones if you need to.

Here are some places that will distribute press releases for free:

- www.prlog.org
- www.pr.com
- www.i-newswire.com
- www.pr9.net
- www.bignews.biz

You can also increase the likelihood that your press release will be picked up by Google News and other top news websites by submitting to a pay service, such as www.prweb.com. For a cost of $40 and up you can receive a significant increase in the effectiveness of your press release. Features include:

- Same day distribution of your press release.
- Upload of graphics and multimedia (graphics are not usually possible with the above free services).
- Inclusion of RSS, XML, OPLM, and NewsML.
- Inclusion into major search engines including Google News, Yahoo News, MSN News, and more.
- Availability of SEO assistance.
- Excellent statistics on the performance of your press release.
- Targeting of as many as 10 industries.
- Free editorial review.

PRWeb Direct also offers valuable tips on their website to help you with press release development and submission. The company is one of the oldest online press release distribution agencies around, with 100,000 contacts, industry analysts and freelance journalists in its databases. It's a great service and well worth checking out.

The other ways to find places that will accept your news item is to search via your favorite search engine like:

"submit press release" or "industry segment"

substituting "industry segment" with your target market. You'll be surprised by the number of places that will accept newsworthy items—after all, it's free content for them!

You can also submit paper copies of your release to any relevant newspapers, magazines or journals, and email copies of it to any webmasters, e-newsletter editors and other places of interest to your target audience. If your story has a local angle, then submit it to your local papers as well.

Press releases are a good way to pre-sell to potential buyers because they build credibility with the reader since most people think of a press release as news.

A free page on Squidoo

As far as free advertising is concerned, this one is a real no brainer. Squidoo is a website that allows you to build as many web pages as you like. And if you sign up for free and build a page on the subject of your eBook, you can then link into your sales page at several points throughout that lens. A lens is the term for a web page on Squidoo.

The best approach is to think about the different areas of your subject, and can build a separate web page on each one. For example, let's say you wrote that eBook about the various ways that you can make money online. You would go to Squidoo and build a separate web page on each method of making money online. And you'd also build one page on the eBook itself.

Squidoo gives you lots of tools for building lenses, and it's worth taking the time to build a lens that is a decent length. It should also be packed with useful information. If your page on Squidoo helps people to get a grip on the subject, they will be much more likely to click through the link you have given them. And that means you might convert more of those readers into buyers.

This method of generating traffic is similar to creating a free eBook to give away. This is a form of pre-selling makes the reader more comfortable with you before you ask them to make a purchase. The more times a person interacts with you the easier a sale becomes, which is called pre-selling.

A word of caution—some people use Squidoo to build very short lenses that basically say 'buy my eBook now!' That's not the best way to use the website, and if you use this method of attracting attention, you will be seen as someone who only wants to make money.

Now that may be one of the driving forces for writing your eBook, but you shouldn't be projecting that image to other people. Remember what we said earlier about focusing on the reader and not yourself? It's good to tell a story about how you came to know what you are telling them in the eBook, but don't focus on yourself.

Squidoo works at best when you use it to form a bridge between yourself and the people out there who are looking for information. Squidoo has a very strong community and a great standing in the Google search engine. This means that if you take the time to build a web page that is packed with information, you will be rewarded with some healthy traffic and a chance of sending quality leads from your lens to your eBook sales page.

It takes time to establish an effective page on Squidoo. When you build it, make sure you don't publish it until it is ready. You can do this by saving your lens as a draft until it's ready to face the world. Even when it's published you can add more content to it and add valuable content to it over time. The best lenses start strong by providing valuable and relevant information and consistent updates.

When you create your first lens, you will see that you have dozens of modules to choose from. Some of these are moneymakers in their own right while others give you more freedom to write what you want to. The text/write module in particular opens up a whole new realm of opportunities. If you know a little bit of html, you'll be surprised at what you can do with this module. EZHTML at www.ezhtml.net is a great website that makes html easy to learn.

Don't feel overwhelmed when you start with Squidoo. There are lots of tutorials available on the internet to walk you through the steps.

In only a short time you will have the skills to set up lens very quickly. You'll also gain an understanding of what makes a great web page. To give you a head start I want to share with you some tips on how to get started.

Read all the following tips and then go and set up your free Squidoo account:

1. **Fill out your profile page.** Every time someone visits one of your lenses, they will see a box in the top corner of the page that tells them who made the lens. In this case, that's you! When you take a look at your profile page, you'll see that you can add a picture as well as give a short description of yourself. Now think carefully before you fill this in, because you want to give people a good impression. Don't tell them what you do for a living—tell them what you write about. If your eBook is about making money online, make sure you include that in your description. Describe yourself as an eBook writer too, which will help people picture you as an author. And don't forget to include a professional looking shot of yourself. Don't be tempted to include a picture of you when you were a kid, digging up the garden. Remember that you are doing this to help create an image, and to sell books. So choose carefully!

2. **Choose a good sub-domain for your lens.** A sub-domain is an extension of the main website. So for example, with Squidoo all your lenses will begin with their web address, which is www.squidoo.com. Your own lens will then be tagged onto that. Make sure it's something you can live with because you cannot change it, so make sure it's spelled correctly! A smart option is to choose the title of your eBook. So you might have something like www.squidoo.com/titleofyourebookhere. And remember to use your keywords whenever possible in your sub-domain for SEO.

3. **Choose a catchy title.** Your title should also be intriguing to make people want to find out more. You can talk directly to people, such as: "Do you want to know how to make money

184

online?" or something similar. The good news is that you can change your title at any time, so don't be afraid to try something to see if it works. You can always change it back again.

4. **Write an interesting and relevant introduction.** The introduction is the first module that people will see when they find your lens. It has a very important role to play. It needs to tell them what they can expect to find in the rest of the lens and it must convince the reader to continue reading. It may include a reason for having written the lens in the first place. There are lots of ways you can do it, but the main purpose is to encourage people to keep on reading. The best way to learn what to write is to review the Squidoo's Top 100 Lenses list and learn how the most successful lenses do it. This strategy works for your entire lens, not just the introduction. Some lenses get hundreds and thousands of visitors a week, so it pays to learn how they do it!

5. **Use images as well as words.** A nicely balanced lens that is appealing to look at will always have images as well as words. Think about the cover to your eBook for example. If you have a nice colorful and very appealing looking cover, make sure you flaunt it by including it on your lens. Many people promote a book using the text/write module. With a little html you can get the image to sit on the left hand side of the page and have the text wrap around it. Not only does it look good, it attracts the eye as well. If you need to get images from somewhere else, you can try www.usa.gov/Topics/Graphics.html, www.IstockPhoto.com, www.SXC.hu, www.freeFoto.com, www.EveryStockPhoto.com, and others that can be found with your favorite search engine. Any restrictions will normally be well posted. You can also add relevant videos from websites such as www.YouTube.com.

6. **Analyze your traffic statistics.** When you open your account with Squidoo, you'll get a dashboard that allows you to see how your lenses are doing. Every time you update your lens

(more about that in a moment) the date of the last update will appear on your dashboard. You can also see whether anyone has rated your lens, and how much traffic you are getting. More importantly you will be able to see where your traffic is coming from. Squidoo pages are often ranked in the search engines rather quickly, which is good news for you. And the better your lens does, the higher it will go in the Squidoo ranking system, which in turn can bring more traffic.

7. **Tag your lenses.** Tags are things that attract people to your lens. When you go in to edit or create a lens, you will see you have a column for tags on the right hand side. There is a primary tag, and then you're allowed as many as forty other tags as well. Any or all of these can be changed, deleted or altered at any time. Incidentally, this is a good way to update your lens, especially in the early days. You can go into the edit mode, add a tag, save your changes and then publish the updated lens again. The more good tags you have, the better your traffic should be. You do need to give it time to develop though.

8. **Update your lens frequently.** Fresh lenses usually receive more traffic. If you don't update it at least every week, then your traffic levels are likely to suffer as a result. But an update doesn't have to mean adding a whole new module. It can mean editing the odd word here and there, or adding a new tag as I mentioned above. Even the smallest changes count, and they will all help to keep your lens fresh in the eyes of the search engines too.

9. **Create incoming links to your lens.** Incoming links (back-links) are enormously valuable for any website, and they will be extremely helpful to you when you are building a worthwhile Squidoo lens too. Some of the methods I have yet to tell you about can help you create those links, so stay tuned for those. But you can, and should, become a member of the SquidU forum too. This is a great place to learn more about what makes a good lens, and to give and get advice as well. And you can cre-

ate a signature that links back to your lens or lenses, meaning that every post you make in a forum will give you an inbound link.

10. **Look for the phrases that visitors are using to find your lens.** On your stats page, you will be able to see when people are finding your lens through the search engines. The stats will also tell you what phrases people are typing into search engines to find you with. If you see a plus and minus sign next to any particular phrase, that means you don't have that phrase as a tag on your lens. Tags can be single words or phrases. So make sure you add them in by clicking on the plus sign. This is especially the case if you can see that more than one person has found you through a particular phrase.

11. **When you have something that works, repeat the formula!** You'll know when your lens starts getting popular. Your ranking will start to rise, you'll get plenty of reader comments and five star votes, and your traffic will start going up as well. When this happens, make sure you use that lens as a template for creating your next one. Don't copy it exactly, but make a list of what's working and ensure that you keep it that way for any more lenses you make.

Can you see how valuable this website can be? Not only in funneling people across to your eBook mini-site, but in helping to establish you as an expert on your subject as well.

That's why you need to start using Squidoo as soon as possible. It's very addictive, but it's worth the effort you need to put in to really reap the potential benefits.

Article marketing strategies

As with all the best, and free, promotional methods you could use, this one takes some time and effort, but it also can generate great results if you know how to do it properly. There is no doubt that article directories can bring in a lot of traffic.

Start by writing a series of articles on the same subject as your eBook. Don't promote the book itself in the article; you can do this in what's called the resource box at the end.

The purpose of writing articles is to promote your eBook, but if you promote it directly in the article, it won't be published. You need to do it carefully and write an article that people will find useful and interesting, helpful, and valuable enough, in fact, that they click on the link you are going to provide them with and find out what else you have to offer.

So what do you write about?

Write about various aspects of the subject that you cover in your eBook. In the example we've been using so far, about making money online, you would write articles from topics in your eBook.

One technique is to rewrite sections of your eBook. Articles for directories vary in length but 300 - 400 words should do the trick; they don't have to be excessively long, just make sure they content provides value to readers.

The goal is for the reader to finish the article and click-through to your mini-site on the link in the resource box.

Many article directories let you have a clickable link in the article itself, but others allow you to link only within the actual resource box at the end. Make sure you read the terms and conditions of each directory thoroughly before you submit anything to them.

How do you write the resource box?

It's essential to make it as compelling as possible. Even if your article is wonderful it won't necessarily encourage people to click on your link. You need to encourage them.

Here are some ideas for doing just that:

- Use an unusual or intriguing fact about your eBook to attract their attention.

- Tell them why they should find out more about it.

- Pose a question as I have done above. It makes people think about how it applies to their own life.

- Tell them about a free eBook or report that you are offering on your mini-site or blog (don't mention a product with a price though).

Here are some examples of resource boxes:

- GOOD – "Mr. B has written several eBooks about making thousands of dollars on eBay. Visit www.his-site.net now to find out more."

- BAD – "Mr. B has written an eBook about selling on eBay that is priced at just $27. Order now from www.his-site.net!"

You can see that the second example is purely a ploy to get a sale, and as such it is guaranteed to turn off anyone reading it. The first example, however, is much better; it tells people that Mr. B has experience of writing eBooks about eBay, and gives more specific information too. It also gives the reader the opportunity to visit the mini-site and see the eBooks for themselves, rather than trying to sell to them directly.

Add one link pointing to your mini-site and a second one to your Squidoo page. You just got double the amount of promotion (and valuable one-way backlinks) for very little extra effort.

You should bear in mind though that the more quality articles you write, the more attention you will get. Some people think that all they have to do is write a single article and submit it to half a dozen directories to get huge floods of traffic to their website.

But it doesn't work that way unfortunately. What you need to do is put some regular effort in and make sure that you are writing at least one article every few days. As the number of articles you submit increases so will the traffic of potential customers to your mini-site.

And that means a lot more cash for you.

Article posting strategy

I said at the beginning of this chapter that this method didn't involve spending any money, and that's correct. That's because you will be sending these articles to article directories, which are basically huge websites full of articles on all kinds of different subjects.

The idea of these websites is that people who have things to promote can write articles with their resource box on the bottom and display them on the website for anyone to read and use. The other side of the deal is that webmasters and other people needing material for websites and newsletters can take any of the articles and publish it without payment to the authors provided they keep the resource box at the end of the article so that the authors get to publicize their website in the process.

It's a win-win situation for both parties, and it means that all you have to do is get your articles onto these article directories, so you can start enjoying some traffic.

Now if you have been online recently you may be aware of the discussion that's going on regarding duplicate content. Some people are raising the concern that submitting the same article to plenty of directories can get you penalized by Google.

The best solution is to post your articles to your blog and wait 48 hours for the search engines to crawl the blog. This will make your articles the original copies as they are the first to be crawled. After 48 hours go to www.ezinearticles.com and post your article there. Wait another 48 hours and then post your article with www.articlemarketer.com to send the article out to thousands of websites.

The point is that your articles are out there to generate traffic. Even if you only submitted your articles to one single article directory, there is nothing stopping a dozen different webmasters from taking those articles and publishing them on a dozen different websites, so personally I wouldn't limit your submissions to a particular directory for this precise reason. It simply doesn't make sense.

Some article directories are better than others, and the list below are the top directories based on volume of traffic listed in order starting with the highest traffic:

- www.ezinearticles.com

- www.ehow

- www.articlesbase.com

- www.buzzle.com

- www.webpronews.com

- www.helium.com

- www.goarticles.com

- www.articlesnatch.com

Many of the top internet Marketers submit manually to these, especially EZineArticles, which provides "Expert Author" banners for your mini-site and blogs to help build credibility and expert status.

For a list of the top 50 article directories, based on web traffic, visit www.vretoolbar.com/articles/directories.php.

Another option if your budget allows is to use an article submission service, but you need to make certain that you use a quality service or your plan could backfire with the search engines. The favorite service among internet Marketing Specialists is www.articlemarketer.com. Article Marketer reaches over 67,246 publishers through 5,910 websites, forums and lists.

Submitting articles to many quality websites with links back to your website (backlinks) is very important for your Google Page Rank and to other search engines. These backlinks are connections from websites all around the internet that guide readers back to your website. Your linking strategy could mean the difference between the success and failure of your online business.

A high quality strategy will provide lots of qualified traffic that will convert at high rates for your newsletter, eBook, and buying other products.

Backlinks are gigantic when it comes to driving tons of traffic to your site because major search engines factor in the quality and number of backlinks in search engine results. So, backlinks increase search engine rank, which can generate more traffic from the search engines.

Submitting your articles

Before you can submit your work, you will need to join each website you want to submit to.

This is easy to do, and while you can sometimes choose your own password some of the websites give you a six digit number to remember, so make sure you either file all the emails away for future reference or make a separate note of your log ins!

Submission is usually quite straightforward, but do make sure you read through all the instructions before you do so, because it will hold you up if you get an article rejected because you made a simple mistake.

You can get article submission software to help speed up the process if you end up submitting your articles to more than a handful of websites; this is available at low cost online now (some people are even giving it away as a thank you or a bonus on some occasions) and although you still have to do certain things manually, it does make filling in forms much easier to do.

The other benefit of submitting to several article directories is that you can create links in the resource box which goes back to your mini-site and blog (or any page on your websites that is appropriate, like a free eBook or report sign-up page). Google loves these backlinks when ranking websites in their search results, so it stands to reason that the more articles you can write and the more sites you can submit them to, the more links you will get as a result.

Regardless of how you submit your articles, you should consider submitting manually to at least www.ezinearticles.com.

While you stand a good chance of getting some traffic from the very first article you submit, you will get better results if you make this a regular activity.

Even if you aren't a natural writer, you will soon get used to writing a short article every now and then. If you can manage one a week, that represents a lot of publicity over the weeks to come, and plenty of links going back to your mini-site and blog.

Make a note in your diary or on your calendar now to write an article every week, and submit it to your list of directories as soon as you are happy with it. This is one of the best ways to get free traffic online today, and the more effort you put into it, the more you will get in the way of rewards as well.

Another option for churning out many articles much faster is to join Private Label Rights (PLR) websites, many of which are free, to access free products that may be related to your niche.

It is quite possible that you can find hundreds of articles already written on you niche topic, all you have to do is rewrite it so that it won't be seen as duplicate content by the search engines (your content needs to be original or the search engines consider it useless and will penalize your blog). Prior to posting any content on your blogs, you should get in the habit of confirming the content is original by going to www.copyscape.com and performing a search for duplicate content on the web. For $5 you can perform 100 searches, which is very inexpensive to ensure original content.

Offering articles elsewhere

You've got another option here too, if you are enjoying the process of writing articles about your subject.

In addition to submitting them to your various article directories, you can also approach webmasters and bloggers directly with the offer of an article (or blog post) about the subject to go on their website or blog.

This can work very well as most people will be only too glad to receive a good piece of writing that is relevant to their audience. All you need to do is offer an article for free, provided your link to your mini-site or blog is included at the bottom of it.

It helps here to make it clear that the article is unique and hasn't been published anywhere else. People will be far more likely to use your piece if they know it is exclusive to them.

The best way to approach this method of promotion is to go into Google—or any other major search engine—and search for websites and blogs that are related to your subject. Make a list of them and contact each one with an offer. You just need to remember that anyone who says yes will require a unique article—so make sure you have plenty of good ideas to use.

Quick delivery of your article or blog post in each case is also a good thing, and it will make it more likely that you can continue the arrangement and write the odd article for them in the future as well. Not only does this give you a great (and free) way to promote your eBook mini-site, it also gives you the opportunity to build bridges and make connections with other people in the business.

If you want additional information on article marketing I recommend Steve Wagenheim's "The Complete Article Writing and Marketing Guide" available at:

www.honestincomeprogram.com/tcawamg.html.

I am not affiliated with, and do not know, Mr. Wagenheim. If you read his posts in www.warriorforum.com you will quickly learn he is a respected, honest, and intelligent internet marketer. What better route to promoting your eBook could there be?

Blogging to get attention

When people talk about blogging, one of the first things you'll hear is how much money you can make by doing it. What you don't hear quite so often is how much publicity it can bring you.

In a round about way of course, blogging for promotional purposes does earn you money, but if you want to make a name for your-

194

self and your products or services online, blogging is one of the best ways that you can do it and that's what we're going to focus on in this chapter.

Some reasons why blogging about niche topics is so successful are:

- Credibility -If a blogger consistently focuses on the blog topic and provides valuable information, you will become seen as a credible source of information, hopefully even an expert. When you create products directly related to this topic, you have a ready market to tap into.

- Search Engine Ranking - Search engines love websites with all webpages directly related to a single topic, and higher search engine placement is made easier with this type of website.

- Improved Conversion Rates (percentage of people who land on your sales page and place an order)—Conversion rates are improved when you build an ongoing relationship with potential customers that consider you a credible expert in the field.

Focus on the right topic

Unlike press releases, where you have to get specific to reach your audience, you need to be a little more general when it comes to blogging. For example, if you have a website that sells eBooks on all kinds of different subjects, then your blog would also be focused on the subject of eBooks—writing them, selling them, making a living from them and so on. You wouldn't focus your blog on just one type of eBook, or writing about them and ignoring the selling aspect completely, because this would narrow your focus too much.

In any event, the different aspects of your online business would be dealt with in different categories on your blog, helping to define what the blog is about and making it easier for people to navigate its contents.

When researching topics for new blogs you should ask yourself some questions:

- Am I interested in the topic? This is important as you will be spending much time writing about this topic each week, for years, and you will need to become an expert in this field.

- Are you an expert in this field or are you willing to become one quickly through research? Remember that you will have to come up with many topics to write about in the coming months and years.

- Is there a market for this topic? This is obviously critical to the long term success of your blog; no interest = no $.

- Use the free trial version of Wordtracker at www.freekeywords.wordtracker.com to determine keywords.

- Is this a growing or dying topic? Make certain that the topics that you consider are increasing in popularity rather than fading away into oblivion. To research search topics and niches check out www.google.com/insights/search for information of niche markets such as seasonal swings of search volume and geographic demographics. Use www.google.com/trends to track the search volume history of specific keywords. Remember that your topic will need to appeal to readers in the future. A possible good topic may be a blog on hurricanes. If scientists are correct, we can expect more hurricanes with increased strength in the future, and this should increase interest in the topic.

- Will you have enough content? Do you know enough about the topic to write weekly for years, or is there enough information available to you for researching new blog topics?

- Will your topic generate money? Certain topics are not good producers of cash. Think about what people are looking for when you are considering a topic. Are people looking for a product to buy (best case scenario as the person is already in the mindset to make a purchase), are people looking for information to assist with making an informed buying decision (also great potential, if you provide this information, then you are positioned to assist with the purchase through an affiliate or your own product), or are the people looking for entertainment (worst type, how many people searching for celebrity gossip are likely to buy a product?)? Also consider which advertisers are paying high pay per click rates for Google AdSense ads (see www.adwords.google.com to learn more). You should use www.adwords.google.com/select/KeywordTool to get a feel for how much advertisers pay for which keywords.

A couple of other tools you should consider using during your search for blog topics include:

- www.google.com/trends - Useful in determining if a niche market is growing or dying.

- www.technorati.com - One of the largest blog search engines. Use this website to determine what others are writing about your niche topic.

- www.blogsearch.google.com - Similar to Technorati.

Getting your blog started

Blog platform choices are wide, but four of the most popular free providers include:

- www.blogger.com - Very basic service hosted on their servers or yours. If you use their servers, they will run ads in around your blog, but you can also run your AdSense ads within the blog. The search engines consider this type of blog less important, so expect less organic traffic from the search engines.

- www.wordpress.com - It is a popular choice among new bloggers as it is open source, free, very easy to use, and has a large community of users, lots of plugins, and three versions to choose from. Resides on their server or yours.

- www.b2evolution.net - It can be installed on your website and includes all the features of traditional blog tools, and extends them with evolved features such as file & photo management, advanced skinning, multiple blogs support as well as detailed user permissions. It is open source, free, and has third party plugins.

- www.nucleuscms.org - It can set up one or more weblogs on your server, and you can even show the contents of multiple weblogs on the same page. They have lots of plugins and documentation to assist with startup.

Create an email signature

This is one of those simple little things that takes around five to ten minutes to set up, but keeps working for you every single day from then on.

And it helps you to spread the word to lots of people as well. The great thing with forwarding emails to people is that the entire email is kept intact. If your email gets forwarded it has your signature on it that means more promotion for you—and for your eBook.

So what is an email signature?

It's a simple way of signing off on every email you send. Most people use it to add something like, "Best wishes, Joe Bloggs", or "Yours sincerely, Joe Bloggs."

But you can add an email signature that promotes your latest eBook instead. You can still sign off in the traditional way if you wish (it does save a lot of time), but underneath that you can put something like this:

"Want to find a way to make $200 extra every single week? Then take a look at my latest eBook, "How to Make Money Online."

And then you would make the title of your eBook into a clickable link so people could just click on it to be taken to your mini-site. Then they can read more about it and perhaps even buy a copy.

The same thing that applies to resource boxes for articles applies here too. You need to make sure that people want to click. Arouse curiosity in people. Make sure they are intrigued by what you are offering. Take a while to experiment with what seems to work and what doesn't.

In fact, if you have been experimenting with those resource boxes for a while already, see which one works better than the others and base your signature on that.

A large percentage of internet users have more than one email account, so make sure you put your signature on every single one of them. This applies even if it is your own personal email account that you use for placing orders with websites and emailing your friends and family! You just never know who is going to read it or think your signature is intriguing enough to click on that link...

In short, this is a simple way to promote yourself that really doesn't take long to set up. And once it is set up, you can forget about it. It takes care of itself. And it doesn't cost a cent to do it. Don't knock that—free promotion is still worthwhile!

Building reputation in forums

The internet is full of forums. There are probably forums out there for virtually every single subject under the sun. And that means there will likely be more than one forum around which is relevant to the subject of your eBook as well.

You need to be careful when you use forums to promote yourself and your eBook. Blatant promotion won't get you anywhere—it will just get you thrown off for spamming its members. You don't want that.

But you can use forums to advertise your eBook if you know how to do it properly.

First up, you need to read the terms and conditions that each forum has. Some of them are quite lenient when it comes to mentioning your own mini-site address, but most of them are dead set against it.

What you need to do is to find out whether you can include your mini-site address in the signature at the bottom of every post you make. If you can, then you won't have to worry. Many forums do in fact allow you to do this: it's promoting your mini-site or blog during the actual post itself that is a real no no.

You also need to be sure you pick the best forums for your needs. If you are writing about saving money, then you need to find forums that concentrate on that subject. If you want to reveal the ways that you have made money online, well there are plenty of forums out there that cover that subject as well.

You'll certainly get the hang of it eventually, but the best course of action is to be cautious and don't promote in any way at all during a forum post.

What type of forum posts should you be writing?

Well you can indulge in two main types, and you should really make the most of using both of them because they will help to integrate you into the forum community more readily.

The first one is to join in conversations that are already going on. This offers you the chance to put across your point of view, but you should always remember to keep a professional outlook. If you disagree with someone, don't be drawn into a dirt slinging match – that's the worst possible outcome you could hope for.

Instead, you need to make sure that you are always polite and courteous. Appreciating that everyone has an opinion is one of the key points to being an active and welcome member of a forum. And if you come across as someone who is less than polite, the best thing is to withdraw from conversing with them. Some people are only intent on getting a rise out of you, and you will never win in that situation; that is, unless you retreat and maintain a dignified and professional outlook, of course.

The second way to contribute is to start off a new topic by posting a new thread in a section of the forum. This can be a good way to start talking with other members as well. Try posing a question that you think other forum members might be interested in, so that you can get a good conversation going. Many people like picking up on new threads to see what the latest talk is all about, so you will naturally get a decent amount of traffic to any conversation that you start.

Just be sure to remain a key part of the conversation the whole way through! There's nothing worse than starting something and then not contributing to the ensuing discussion.

You should also bear in mind that becoming a regular is one of the best ways to get a good response from this type of marketing. You'll notice when you join that you will be able to see how many posts you have made next to your screen name. That means you (and everyone else) can instantly see whether you are an active member or not.

And you can be sure that active members tend to be listened to and receive a bit more attention than those that come in at the beginning, make a lot of posts and then disappear for months on end. Regular efforts are the key to getting traffic from this source. People will keep coming across your name, and they'll start to become familiar with you and what you have to say. And that means there will be an increasing chance that they will hop over to your eBook mini-site to see what else you've been up to.

It's said that the majority of people won't buy the first time they see something new for sale. There are exceptions of course, but they will quite often hang back or not even register the product to begin with. They need to see the advert or link a few times before they click on it to see what it's all about.

That means that a half hearted attempt to make contact with a new audience initially might get a couple of responses, but it won't get the sales you are looking for. It's the constant and determined efforts that really bring the rewards.

This applies to everything I am revealing to you in this chapter. You might feel as if you are doing a lot of activities and not really seeing any results from them yet. Don't worry—that's quite normal. Think of it as being the same as taking antibiotics when you have a throat infection—it will still hurt for the first few days, but then it gets into your system and you really notice a difference!

I know that's a strange example to use, but it does illustrate that there are things going on when you start to promote your eBooks using all these different methods. You just need to keep on doing them for a longer amount of time if you want to get the best possible results from them all.

Other possibilities

And if that wasn't enough to keep you occupied, here are some other ways and means you can use to get your eBook out there and in front of as many eyeballs as possible.

Remember, you don't have to try all of these, and you don't have to try to get involved in everything from the word go. Dip into one or two at a time and make the most of them before introducing another method of getting traffic. Once you get the hang of one you can expand your free marketing methods in other directions—never forgetting, of course, that you need to keep your hand in with the ones you've already started.

Using social networking websites

If you don't have a membership with any social networking websites yet, now is the time to make a start.

You don't need to join all of them, but you can certainly get some good results by getting involved with one or two and connecting with people who are going to enjoy what you have to offer.

The same rules that apply to forums apply here—most will object to direct promotion so don't do it. If you think of the other members of these websites as being people instead of customers, you won't go wrong.

And make sure you explore before joining any single website. There are lots of them available and some will appeal to you more than others. If you are going to make this worthwhile, you'll need to enjoy what you're doing, so find the website that fits you the best.

Bookmarking your website as a favorite

Along with social networking websites, there are social bookmarking websites as well. And you can share your favorite websites with other members, so why not share your Squidoo lenses, your blog and of course your eBook mini-site as well?

And when you consider that you can also bookmark all the articles you write for the article directories, that can provide a lot more links and a lot more traffic overall than you would have otherwise.

You'll find a list of the best social bookmarking websites in the Resource section at the back of this eBook, along with a list of social networking websites as well. Refer to this when you are ready to get started in this department.

Get involved because there are lots of benefits to doing so—but make sure you know what you're getting into first.

Try a different tack—make use of YouTube

Lots of people have benefited from this. It's not a social networking website as such—it's really in a league of its own.

But if you are good at making short videos, you will love this website. Instead of writing articles to promote your eBook, you can film yourself giving advice on the subject instead. You will get a user page as well that people can look at... with room for your mini-site or blog address. And people can subscribe to your videos so they won't miss any of them in future. That's ideal if you want to build up a following.

Quick tip – a lot of people who are quite successful on YouTube make use of running a series of videos. If people watch a short video and see that it is one of six, for example, they will automatically look for the other five, if they like it.

And while you cannot directly promote on YouTube, you will notice that a lot of people take steps to make sure their website address is included in the bottom right hand corner of the screen for the entire video.

And since a good video with the right keywords in the title will generally get a lot of views (often in the thousands) over time, that address could be seen by rather a lot of people, wouldn't you say?

So maybe it's time to make your face famous as well as your name, and of course your eBook!

Registering your eBook wherever you can

There are some websites that allow you to list your eBook free of charge. You may not get a lot of visitors this way, but each one will certainly give you another valuable inbound link to your mini-site, so they are worth doing.

A good example of these types of sites is one called BookHitch. This website markets itself as a 'search engine for books', and it enables people to find a book on any subject using its search facility.

Some of the services it offers have to be paid for, but you can easily list your eBook for free so you don't have to pay anything if you don't want to.

There are a couple of other similar websites which give you the same benefits. The following list has been compiled to give you a one stop resource for all the websites you will need to help you get your own eBook up and running;

- www.ebookscafe.writergazette.com/addbook.php (associated with Writer Gazette)

- www.ebook2u.com

- www.ebookjungle.com

- www.jogena.com

- www.virtual-ebooks.com/addabook.htm

- www.ebooksubmit.com

Keep an eye out for any other websites that allow you to list your book for free, and make sure you do it as soon as you spot them.

They'll never do you any harm, and you might make a sale or two out of them, as well as that free link back to your mini-site.

The more links you get, the stronger your mini-site is likely to be in the eyes of Google and the other search engines. And the higher you can get in those results, the better off you will be. For SEO you need to include your sales page main keyword/phrase in the directory listing, as early as possible such as in the ad title. That will improve the relevancy of your backlink.

So you can see there are plenty of ways that you can promote your eBook and make more sales in the process. Once you get going you might even want to set up your own blog to connect with your readers a bit more. And once you have some money coming in, you can allocate a certain amount towards paid advertising such as Google AdWords for example.

But many eBook sellers find that once their website gets indexed and their free articles start to find their way across the web, they don't even need to pay for any advertising. All of which means more profit for you!

Chapter 15:
Easily Sell Your Books in Bookstores

Most major eBook sellers will tell you that your best bet is to set up an individual mini-site for each eBook that you want to sell. That is certainly the best way. But it makes sense to maximize your chances of selling as many copies as possible, and that's why you need to make sure you look at other possibilities for selling it.

And that's what we're going to do in this chapter—including taking a look at selling hard copies as well.

Selling your eBook on Lulu.com

Lulu is probably the best known and most successful website that is geared up to help people like you self publish and sell their books.

The great thing about Lulu is that there is no charge to put your eBook online. Once someone buys a copy, Lulu takes its cut and the remainder of the cover price (which you set yourself) goes into your account. And they will pay via PayPal too, so it's all nice and easy.

Lulu adds 25% to whatever price you decide to sell your eBook for, so bear this in mind when you figure out your selling price. Let's say for example that you want to receive $10 for each copy you sell. Lulu would add $2.50 to that sum (25% of $10 is $2.50), so the final selling price would be $12.50.

You might need to experiment with some different prices to make sure you get the result you want, but since Lulu doesn't charge you for the privilege of using the website, this is a very pleasant split between them and you for every copy you sell.

You can also choose to sell your eBook completely free of charge if you wish. Remember what I mentioned about selling a freebie to encourage more interest in the real thing? Well you could certainly do that here if you wanted to. Just make sure that the freebie is worthwhile and offers real value, so that people will cross over to your mini-site to find out more about the paid version.

Print on demand (or POD)

Print on demand, or POD, publishing might sound like something from outer space, but it is quite a simple process and what's more it can make your eBook even more attractive to potential buyers.

So how does it work? Well, whether you like it or not, not everyone likes eBooks. Plenty of people do, but there are also plenty of people who prefer to have a solid book in their hands instead of reading it on their computer.

In the past, if you wanted to transform your eBook into a proper printed volume, you would have had to spend a few hundred dollars on a set number of books up front. Most printers had (and still have, in some cases) a minimum print run, which means that you can only reduce your costs so far; if you don't sell your book, and it doesn't prove to be as popular as you thought it might be, then you could end up with a garage full of books that end up gathering dust for months and years to come.

Print on demand does away with this danger. Let's suppose you go down this route with Lulu, for example. You can still sell your eBook as an eBook, but you will also be able to offer it for sale as a standard book. You upload your manuscript as an eBook, and it's ready for download as soon as someone buys it in that format.

But what happens when someone wants to buy it as a standard paperback book?

Lulu print on demand

What you need to do is to make it available in this format to begin with. This is very easy to do, thanks to the wealth of information and advice that Lulu gives you in its help section. Check out the Lulu section on formatting on their website at www.lulu.com/en/help/book_formatting_faq. This is broken down into stages so that you can easily access the parts you need. You can also pay Lulu to perform the editing for you and prices range from $200 for light editing to $500 for heavy editing.

Lulu also provides design prices for covers at www.lulu.com/en/services/marketing/covers.php?cid=en_services_l eftnav_custom_cover where prices range from $80 for a custom eBook cover to $1,000 for a deluxe cover. The only thing to bear in mind with print on demand via Lulu is that you have the cost of actually printing the book to think about. There are still no upfront charges though – you won't have to pay a thing until you make a sale. Check out their demo at the website www.lulu.com/en/about/demo.php?cid=en_tab_demo. You can also see what they charge to print books at www.lulu.com/en/products/paperback/?id=en_home_publish, just scroll down and the pricing tool is on the right.

At the time of writing Lulu has broken down the fees into two main types. First, there is a flat fee which they call a base cost. This is the same regardless of the type or size of book you want to publish. Second, there is a printing cost, which varies depending on how many pages your book has, and whether they are in color or black and white. Basically this is a flat fee per page, which is made in cents.

Lulu itself still takes a cut of the proceeds from each sale, but as with eBooks when you make a sale, you will simply receive your portion of the cover price in your account. Simple, right? And if there is anything you aren't sure about, you can bet that Lulu will have answered your question already in their help section. Lulu also has a live help facility where you can speak to someone directly if you need to.

There's also plenty of info about ISBN's as well (remember those?), and it will benefit you to read it. If you just want to make a hard copy of your book available on Lulu, then you don't need to worry about getting one if you don't want to, but as we found out before, it is necessary if you want it available to 60,000 bookstores and libraries including Amazon and Barnes and Noble so that anyone can find out about it. You can also sell your products on CD through Lulu.

And since I'm assuming you want to be selling as many copies of your books as possible, you'll probably be only too pleased to do whatever is necessary to make that happen.

BookSurge print on demand

It doesn't take much reading to find out that BookSurge is part of that huge bookstore you might have heard of—Amazon.

In many ways it is very similar to the services offered by Lulu, but for those people who are less able to create a PDF that is ready to be printed exactly as it is, it may be of more use.

The one thing to remember with BookSurge is that there are upfront prices to be paid. You'll be looking at shelling out a few hundred dollars even for this most basic of services.

Once you are all set up and ready to publish your book, you'll get 35% of sales, which is a whole lot more than you'd get if you wanted to publish your book through a traditional publisher. And that's assuming that you'd even get one interested in the first place.

The first step to getting your hardcover or paperback book published through this website is to fill in the online form. They will then contact you to find out more about your project, and you go ahead from there.

BookSurge can be a good bet if you definitely want to move on from the eBook world. We've seen how beneficial it is to publish eBooks, but there is no doubt that publishing it as a hard copy as well will open you up to even more customers both now and in the future. Some people don't really think about a book as being real unless it has a cover on it!

As well as having a bookstore section on this website, BookSurge also has a number of other websites on which your book will be sold, including Amazon. So while there are upfront costs involved here, there are also plenty of benefits too.

If this all seems very overwhelming and the thought of publishing your book in solid form is too expensive to bear right now, don't worry. Focus on getting your eBook sorted out and published, and sell as many copies of it as you can via your mini-site, and perhaps Lulu as well.

Once you start to get the money rolling in, you can use some of it to invest in more services at BookSurge. Don't feel like you have to do everything at once, because it can be done in stages if you wish. It all depends on how you want to approach it. What's more, running with your eBook initially at the lowest cost possible will let you gauge whether or not it is going to be worth publishing in a big way. It might get with the right kind of reception, or it could be that your audience for it isn't as big as you thought it might be.

Take things one step at a time—you might find it easier that way.

Lightning Source print on demand

Lightning Source is owned by the company that owns the biggest book wholesaler in the US, Ingram Book Group. If you use Lightning Source for your POD needs, then Ingram will always list your book as "in stock". This means that your book becomes immediately available in Ingram's catalog to almost all bookstores in the US and many around the world (they have print shops in several countries).

If you work with Lightning Source, you can receive much more revenue from the sale of each book compared to Lulu and BookSurge with the proper strategy. One thing you need to know is that Lighting Source doesn't work with authors, only publishers. They are too big to spend time holding author's hands.

This is not a problem though, if you already have a company great, if you don't, start one and call it something Publishing, Inc. or Media, LLC (but don't use your name for your business name, make it sound like a professional company).

Amazon pulls book information directly from the Ingram catalog so your title will automatically be listed on Amazon as in stock or available in 24 hours. And if your book sells several copies in a short period of time, Amazon is likely to purchase in bulk directly from Lightning Source and stock them in their warehouses around the US.

Other giant booksellers are set up electronically with Lightning Source, which bypasses Ingram and potentially allows them to purchase your book in bulk at a discount that meets their needs. Typically you will need to offer a 40% discount to the seller to attract attention in the hope of getting your book on the book shelves of the brick and mortar stores.

You need to set up an account with Lightning Source. You need to purchase an ISBN and you can refer back to the chapter at the beginning of this book for more information about an ISBN number and the benefits it brings, and you'll also find the website you need for more details on how to get one when you look in the resources section at the back of this book.

If you have your own mini-site up and running, then your eBook will no doubt already be raring to go in PDF format. That's great, but Lightning Source, Lulu, and BookSurge need to receive the file in PDF format (use Adobe's software or you may have font issues).

Optimize your book for print on demand

The optimum page count for a book printed by Lightning Source is just over 100 pages and no more than 200 (50 pages is the minimum page count Lightning will print). This is one more reason to write concisely to jam as much value packed information into those 100 plus pages. If the content is valuable, you can price the book at what it is worth, and the higher the price the better.

The printing machines are designed for optimum black text and no pictures. It is advisable to only include simple single color drawings or none at all. Keep it simple.

Typical trim size is 6" x 9"

Don't use free PDF converters for POD

If you are going through the effort to get a professionally written book into print, you should not chance the free PDF converters at this critical point of the publishing process. Free PDF converters may miss some of the more intricate symbols, graphics, characters, etc. But guess what, you can still use the best in the business for free for one month. You can sign up for your free online Beta version of Adobe Acrobat PDF Converter at www.acrobat.com/#/cpdf/CreatePDFBegin.

It might also be advisable to give it the once over before you submit it, just to make completely sure that you are happy with everything. Don't forget that this is going to be available through Amazon and most other booksellers, and it is going to represent you as a writer as well, so make the most of it! If you are printing with Lightning Source you should know that they want publishers to use the process in 'Properly publishing your eBook in PDF' on page 25.

The actual process of joining Lightning Source is very easy. You just need to go through the step by step process of uploading your document to its website using the instructions given. They've also got a downloadable PDF document of their own that tells you all about creating a publishable digital document, so be sure to read it if you need help.

The most important thing is to remember that your document needs to be ready for the printers. Refer back to page 25 for the process of converting your file to meet Lightning Source requirements.

So with that simple operation done, what happens next?

Er, nothing. In fact all you need to do now is wait for the sales to start coming in, courtesy of Amazon and a few other major websites that Lightning Source promotes their catalog of eBooks with. You won't see your eBook on Amazon within minutes of publishing it through Lightning Source though – you should give it a few days for that to happen, as it will need to go through its own part of the process to complete the whole thing.

Of course, it does help if you can promote your book independently. A bit of positive promotion never hurt anyone and it can certainly increase sales. The best thing you can do is to tell as many people as possible that your eBook can be found on Amazon. And of course, having that all important ISBN number will help enormously.

You will, of course, be giving a portion of the price of your eBook to Amazon, but when you can get your eBook onto a website that has traffic in the millions every month, why would you worry about that? This is a new avenue of sales for you to go down, and it is well worth making the journey.

Benefits and drawbacks

Let's take the benefits first. The costs involved to get your eBook on Amazon are minimal—especially when you compare them to the volume of sales you could get for a good book.

You'll also get your eBook in front of a wider audience than you could ever hope to do elsewhere. You might manage to create a great mini-site that brings in the traffic—but that traffic might be a fraction of what Amazon can offer.

It also makes your eBook more visible elsewhere. Simply having an ISBN number can make things so much easier. And you will be able to keep an eye on how well your eBook sales are doing, thanks to the data that is provided to you by Lightning Source itself.

So are there actually any drawbacks to this venture?

Well, you could say that having to discount your eBook by as much as 50% is a drawback. But then there is a chance that you will make more money from your sales on Amazon than you would from your sales on your mini-site, which of course will bring you 100% of revenue. And since Amazon sales are an added bonus, anything you sell over and above recouping the cost of getting an ISBN number and listing it on the website in the first place is pure profit.

And that really is the only downside!

So give careful consideration to getting your eBook onto Amazon. If you decide not to do it, ask yourself why. If it is because you feel a bit daunted at the thought of getting involved with such a huge company, don't be—because Lightning Source (or any other digital fulfillment company you choose to use) does pretty much all the hard work for you.

All you need to do is sit back and enjoy the proceeds.

What to do with your hard copies

So we've discovered that you can sell hard copies of your book online, through bookstores as big as Amazon. Is there really anything else left to do with them?

Well, yes, actually there is.

Here are some ideas that should get you thinking. But don't view them as being the 'be all and end all' of the possibilities that are open to you. They are simply a way to start you thinking about all the different methods you could use to sell more copies of your book.

So try these for size:

Try local bookshops direct

When you've got your beady eyes on Amazon, it's easy to forget your local bookstore. You might not even think it's worthwhile asking them if they would be interested in stocking your book.

But don't be so sure. Bookstores may be more interested in stocking your book purely because you are a local author. If they can see that there has been a reasonable amount of interest in the title, then you could be onto a good thing.

If you decide to call on a bookstore unannounced, make sure you take at least one copy with you for them to look at. This can actually be the best approach to make, since you get the chance to be more personable. Think about this for a moment—if someone calls you and you don't know them, you automatically think of it as a cold call and put the phone down.

But if you are met with someone face to face, there is more chance of you at least hearing the person out. And if that person is you, and you're trying to get your book onto the shelves of your local independent bookstore, then you might just succeed.

Offer a discount to a specific magazine

If you've done your homework—and I'm assuming by now that you have—you will know that your book falls into a specific category. It appeals to a certain audience.

That means that you will have a pretty good idea of where these people congregate and what magazines and newspapers they read. Now ideally you want to find a specialist magazine that appeals to

215

these people. If you do, you have a ready made audience to sell your books to.

What you want to do is write to the editor and tell him/her all about the special offer you have for his/her readers. This should get his/her attention.

Offer autographed copies

This can make any type of book more attractive to a bookstore – and it can also make it more likely for your book to get a great position among the many other books that are for sale.

Booksellers know that signed copies can sway book sales; someone who is considering buying a book will very likely buy it from the store that can offer a signed copy instead of a standard one.

You can offer signed copies in two ways—first, you could sign a limited number of copies in advance and simply hand them to the bookstore that has agreed to stock your books for you. The other alternative you have is to do a proper book signing, which involves showing up at the bookstore at a pre-arranged date and time, to sign books for people on the spot. The only downside of this is that you never quite know what to expect. Famous name authors will have people lined up around the block, but if you are a total unknown, you may not get anyone turning up at all.

If you agree to do this, the best bet is not to rely on the bookstore to do all the publicity ahead of time. Do some of it yourself too. Get the local paper involved if you can. Tell them who you are, where you live and when you are doing the book signing.

Get all your friends and family to spread the word as well. You should write a press release too (remember those?) to make sure that everyone is aware of the fact that you will be available to sign copies of your book.

In short, don't just expect people to turn up. Make as big a show of it as you can, and you're more likely to be rewarded with more sales and more books to sign.

Give talks at appropriate meetings

How good are you at speaking in front of groups of people? If you like the idea, this opens up another avenue of book selling that could prove to be quite lucrative.

The idea is to approach groups and societies who will have an interest in your book. So for example, let's say you have written a book about photography. What you would do is to approach various photographic organizations and local amateur photography groups. Ask them if they would be interested in having a guest speaker on the subject of your book.

Because you will be offering your services for free, most of them will probably be very interested in the offer. All you need to do is tell them that you have a book for sale and in return for the free talk; you can have a display of your book available so that people can buy a copy at the end if they wish.

It's a good idea to offer signed copies as well if anyone wants them—and if you are willing to drop the cover price by a dollar or so, then so much the better. The idea is to make the offer look very attractive to the group you are approaching—which it will, since you are offering your services free of charge.

If you approach plenty of groups and organizations in this way, you can expect to get several people taking up your offer. And of course there is no limit to the number of times you can give a different talk to the same group. Some people need to see a book several times before they choose to buy, so don't be afraid of going back more than once.

The other advantage of doing this is that you will have the opportunity to make some strong connections in the area of interest your book covers. If you have a mini-site or blog, say so—take this as your opportunity to make as many connections as you can, because they could help you in the future as well as now.

In fact, if you want to get more traffic going to a personal blog (some people have these to tell people about themselves, as well as to announce their latest book releases and reveal links to those sales pages) or a blog, why not have some bookmarks made up to give away with your books? They can have your mini-site address and blog address printed on them, and if you have the ability to print onto card, then you can save some cash by creating them yourself.

You won't have everyone saying yes to your offer, but you should get enough to make this exercise worthwhile. And it always pays to get to know other people in your line of interest. If nothing else, it will give you ideas for future books on the same subject.

Suggest articles to editors

The best tactic to use in this instance is to approach them in writing. And we're not talking about writing articles for website directories here—we're talking about writing articles for 'proper' magazines. The kind you'd find in your local bookstore or newspaper outlet.

Now most editors will pay for any articles they publish. But you want to have details of your book at the end of the articles that you write—because, of course, you want to make some sales.

What you can do is offer an article to them free of charge, on the condition that you can promote your book at the end of it. You can mention that you are prepared to knock a dollar or two off the cover price for their readers in a special deal if you wish—it might just sway the decision; in you favor.

It's important to remember that the article needs to be of good quality and worthwhile. No editor will publish it if it doesn't meet up to his/her usual high standards.

In short, if you can fit in with what they like and how they like it, you will be far more likely to succeed.

Set up a stall at a local fair or book sale

You probably won't get a huge reaction from a book sale or yard sale, but if you are going there anyway, why not take a few of your books with you and set up a small area to promote them?

Be prepared to talk to people about the topic of the book and have your eBook mini-site address displayed as well, in case they want to buy it online.

The key here is to make yourself as well known as possible. Selling hard copies of your book yourself means getting out there and making contacts, so get going!

Don't forget eBay

And the other online auction websites that are around.

If your eBook is on a popular subject and you have some hard copies lying around that you want to get out there and sell, why not stick them on an auction website?

Some of them have charges, while one or two others are free to use and list items on. It doesn't take long to sign up for an account if you haven't already got one, and provided you make the best of your listing you might be able to sell a few copies this way too.

In short, the more you can do to push those book sales, the better. To learn more you should consider picking up Steven Weber's "Plug Your Book!" His book is great resource for promoting your book using online marketing strategies.

Chapter 16:
Promoting Your EBook Offline

The one thing we haven't discussed to any real extent in this book yet is the idea of promoting your eBook offline. We've started to touch on that just now, with the idea of getting your articles published in magazines and the like, but there are other ways that you can sell more books too, without the need to have hard copies to sell.

For example, once you have got the mini-site up and running which sells your eBook, you will have that mini-site address to promote. So while you are doing everything you can to plaster that address across the internet, why not do the same offline as well?

That's the purpose of this section. It should give you some good ideas for getting that mini-site address known and seen by people, even when they aren't online.

Business cards

Who says that business cards have to promote a specific business?

With some thought and planning you can design a business card that promotes your eBook and the mini-site it is sold from. The best idea is to make sure that the best selling points of that eBook are bulleted on the card. You could even splash out a bit more money and have a double sided card.

The idea is to make your business card worth keeping. So you could put some useful information on the back, such as a calendar for the forthcoming year for example.

If you can put a small version of the eBook cover on the front of the business card, it will certainly catch the eye more readily. Of course, having a full color, double sided card will be the most expensive option, but it will also get the most attention and be more likely to be kept for the future. So you may end up making sales long after you hand out some of these cards.

The most important thing to remember is this. If you decide to have your book in eBook form only, you won't have a solid copy that you can carry around with you to show people. So instead, you need to carry around something else. Business cards are perfect because they tuck neatly into your pocket and you can hand them to anyone who asks what you do. Don't tell them about your full-time job—tell them about your writing. I can't tell you how much more interested they will be!

There aren't many people who have published a book in any form, so if you tell them about it and give them a card, they will certainly remember you.

Shop around online for your cards though; some companies will supply them free of charge—you only have to pay for shipping. A classic example of this is VistaPrint, and you'll find their web address in the resources section at the back of the book.

Vista Print offers an amazing online service where you can build all your corporate stationary, stunning business cards, fridge and car magnets, websites, and much more. The system is completely automated and the product shows up at your door. I have used this service often, including business cards for each website.

Car magnets

You've probably seen these on vehicles locally already. They are a lot cheaper than having a paint job done on your car, and the best part is that you can take them on and off as and when you want to. You can get a magnet made up to go on the trunk of your car, or have two done and put one on each door.

The main thing to remember here is that your mini-site address needs to be nice and big so people can read it. The temptation is to put too much on the signs, but remember that people may only have a limited amount of time to read them, so don't make things too complicated.

What you want is for people to go and check out your mini-site, so make sure that it is desirable for them to do so. Try to think of a catchy and intriguing one line sentence to put above the mini-site address itself.

For example, if your eBook is about making money online, you could write something like this:

Want to make $300 extra each week?

Visit www.yourwebsiteaddresshere.com

It's quick, simple and it gets the job done—and that's exactly what you want. Don't fall into the trap of wanting to tell people all about your eBook. Your mini-site is there to do that. You just have to bait the hook to get them there.

Free online ads

A great place to post free information on quality websites is Kijiji.com (or .ca or whichever country is appropriate) and post information about your product and include a link to your mini-site. Remember to bump or repost your ad frequently to keep it in front of as many viewers as possible.

Another popular website that I am sure you have heard of is Craig'sList.com. You can post an ad in your country, state/province, or city and if you are energetic, you can post as many.

Another popular website is www.usfreeads.com where you can post free or paid ads.

Flyers

This won't work for every type of eBook. It really depends on the subject matter.

Let's say, for example, that you have written that book on photography we mentioned earlier. Now you could go to the average street and post a flyer through each door and only hit two or three houses where someone in that household is interested in photography. That's a lot of flyers to waste on people who aren't interested.

But if you go to a meeting which is packed with people who are interested in photography, you could hand out flyers there (with permission) and be guaranteed that they will pretty much all take a look at your mini-site.

But supposing your eBook is about something more generic that more people will be interested in? Making money online, maybe? In this case you would definitely be in with a chance of generating some interest if you handed flyers out or stuck them through doors.

This isn't for the faint hearted, but if you fancy getting out and about, it could be worth a try.

Noticeboards

If you get a few of those flyers made up, why not think about adding them to all the noticeboards you can think of?

It's pretty cheap to get them displayed in shop windows, and some might even let you do it for free. Sometimes giving someone a complimentary copy of your eBook can seal the deal...

But once again, think about how to reach your specific audience. If it's photographers, go to the local meetings and make sure your flyer or poster is promoted there. If you've written a book about animals, you could try local pet stores and vets. I'm sure you can see where this is going; the idea is to be as creative as you can and get your notices in as many places as possible, where you think they would do some good.

It also helps to keep a few in your car, if you have one. You never know when you might get chatting to someone who is more than happy to display your flyer for you. And instead of having to remember to go back with one, it's far easier to pop out and bring it straight in!

Newspaper ads

Ads in newspapers and magazines can work very well—but once again they need to be properly targeted.

You've got two basic types of advertisements to choose from, and these will apply to pretty much every publication you read. They are classified ads and display ads. Classified ads are also sometimes called lineage ads.

Classifieds are paid for by the word usually, so you need to make every word count. You might find that you only have twenty or thirty words to use, so don't just go for the first thing you think of. Spend some time writing a good classified that will really get peoples' attention.

Display ads come in several sizes, and not surprisingly they usually cost a lot more too. You need to weigh up whether the cost is worth it, and how many sales you are likely to make from it as a result.

The best bet is to try classified ads first, and make sure you only take them out in magazines and newspapers that are directly related to the subject of your eBook.

Conclusion

So there you have it—loads of ideas and possibilities when it comes to promoting a hard copy of your book, and also for promoting your eBook offline.

You might be feeling a bit overwhelmed by all this information and all these possibilities, but don't worry too much. Once your eBook mini-site is live and you start getting traffic coming towards it, the best bet is to concentrate on building sources of traffic to begin with. As soon as you start to get some visitors, you can think about using other methods of getting in touch with your audience.

The trick is not to try to attempt too much at once. Pick a method you like (I would recommend getting your eBook active and available with Amazon for starters), and get that sorted out to begin with. You can then go on and pick one more method at a time and see how it works for you.

If it works, you can keep it going, and if it doesn't, then you know you tried. Some methods work better for certain subjects.

The other thing to remember is that you don't have to try all the methods I have described. For example, you may have broken out in a cold sweat at the thought of standing up and giving a talk about your eBook—even if it is a subject you love passionately.

That's okay! Don't feel you have to force yourself into doing things that you know you will hate. If you're not someone who likes standing up in front of a crowd, then forcing yourself into it to try and sell books won't work. People will sense that you don't want to be there—and that isn't the feeling you want them to be getting.

So make sure you are always in control of your promotion, and the rest will take care of itself.

Conclusion:
Getting Started

It seems ironic that the conclusion of this book should be called "Getting Started", but it seemed like the best title for this part of the book.

You see, there are so many people who will reach this page having read the entire contents of the book, who will be fired up to write that eBook that has been buzzing around in their head for ages.

But sadly only a very small percentage of them will actually go ahead and do it. Are you going to be one of them?

I hope that you are, because the potential that lies in this form of publishing is immense. Even without the idea of selling what you have written on Amazon, the potential to make a living that surpasses anything you may have earned so far is huge.

It is up to you what you make of that potential. Many people will reach this stage with dreams, ideas and goals... and yet they will get no further on the road to success. Their greatest ideas and eBooks will be started tomorrow... and of course, tomorrow almost never comes in this situation.

That's why I want to urge you to take that first step <u>now</u>, while everything you have read is fresh in your mind. Don't let typical daily tasks crowd in again just yet—think about what you have read here and decide whether you are going to act on the information in this book, or whether it simply provided you with a way to pass the time and dream about what could be for a while.

If you are determined to improve your life, then you will certainly want to forge ahead right now. You need to ask yourself where you want to be in a year from now. Do you want to be in the same position you are in right now, with the only difference being that this eBook is collecting electronic dust waiting to be read again?

Or do you want to be an author who has at least one eBook completed and making sales steadily throughout every month of the year?

The choice is yours, and I know which choice I would make if I were in your shoes. It is not difficult if you follow the steps in bite size chunks. And once write and sell an eBook once the process becomes much faster.

Planning ahead

That's the secret to building a career in this business. And make no mistake: you CAN make it a career if you want to. There have been plenty of people already who have turned a casual writing experiment into a fully fledged career.

But the one thing that all these people have in common is that they have planned for this to happen. They may have started off with one individual eBook and done very well with it, but from then on they have planned for future eBooks to be written and published. They haven't just fallen out of the sky.

You might hold a dream of being a successful eBook author with dozens of eBooks to your name. You might also dream of being able to look your name up on Amazon and getting dozens of results back in return.

You can do all this if you follow all the advice I have given you in this book. Be sure to keep reading it and keep it close to hand whenever you go through a new stage in the process of writing and publishing your first eBook.

Of course it's easy to spend too much time thinking ahead and dreaming about what might be. Your priority should always be to get that first eBook written and out there, to gauge what the response should be. Thinking about things is perfectly fine, but you need to be dong as well.

So make sure you allocate regular time for your eBook writing. Even if you can only manage a half hour a day, that's a whole fourteen hours over the space of four weeks that you can devote to writing your first eBook. And believe me, once you have completed the whole process once, you'll be itching to do it again!

Your first eBook is just the start

Never forget that the potential here is huge. It doesn't matter whether you want to create a business around publishing small eBooks on a regular basis, according to a pattern you have set up, or you want to publish one eBook every six months. You can write as many as you want to, but just remember that they all start in the same place.

They all start with ideas. Good ideas. Ideas that you can work with.

If there is one caveat to all this that I would like to end on, it is this. Don't fall into the trap of thinking that you know everything there is to know about the eBook business. There are always new things to learn.

It can happen that someone will write and publish his/her first eBook and generate good sales for it in return. Then he/she thinks they've aced the process and charge straight into book number two.

But therein lies the danger. If you aren't careful, it's very easy to make a crucial mistake and forget about some of the steps involved in the research process you must go through before you start writing.

If that happens, you could end up wasting many hours writing a book that just won't sell, no matter what you do.

So always make sure you follow the process I have outlined in this book.

On that encouraging note, I wish you the very best of luck with your eBooks.

Although of course, as we have already seen, once you know what you are doing and how to write these books in the first place (and who to write them for), you will find that luck isn't involved quite as much as you might previously have thought.

This process changes often so I strongly advise you to sign up for updates. You can receive the updates and the simple to follow action plan and the video tutorials and other resources at www.writeandsellebooksguide.com/blog.html.

Remember to take small steps and you will have your eBook for sale electronically and in print in no time. Please send me an email at scottboyd@globoticmedia.com when your book is for sale on Amazon and I will be one of your first customers!

Glossary

Advert – an advert is a way of advertising a product or service. The term 'advert' is more commonly used in relation to traditional print publishing (i.e. newspapers and magazines) rather than online publishing, although it is sometimes used in this arena as well. Adverts come in two main forms, classifieds and display ads (see separate entries in this glossary for these). The size for these varies, and different publications may offer different set sizes.

Affiliates – this is the term given to people who make a living (part-time or full-time) from selling products that have been created by other people. They do not handle the product directly; instead they will send traffic to a website through their own unique URL. The website owner then makes a record of this and sends the affiliate a proportion of any sales that are made through their link.

Amazon – this is a major website which sells, among other things, books. It is of particular interest to eBook writers because it allows you to sell your own books on their site. This can be done through print on demand companies such as Book Surge and Lightning Source (see separate entry, and also the entry in the Resources section).

Article directory – an article directory is a website that is dedicated to housing thousands of articles which are royalty free. That is, they can be used by anyone on any website, provided the resource box (see separate entry) that is added to the bottom by the author of the article is not removed. The articles are written for free in exchange for the publicity and inbound links (see separate entry) that they bring.

Auction sites – these are websites that allow people to list items for sale for a low fee or for free. People can then bid on the item and the highest bid wins. Some authors sell a number of their own books in this way, and it can also be a good way to get a higher profile in a new area.

Author – the term given to the writer of a book. This applies to eBooks as well, although you will more often see them referred to simply as writers, when the product is self published online.

Base cost – this refers specifically to part of the pricing structure brought in by Lulu (see separate entry) to charge for books that are published with them using the print on demand method (see separate entry). This part of the cost covers the basic items required for publishing that do not differ between books, no matter what size they are. It is also referred to as a fixed cost.

Blog – a blog is a weblog, or an online diary. It is much more personal than a website since the writer will give their thoughts and ideas on a subject. In more recent years writers have been using blogs to promote their eBooks, as well as numerous other websites or interests they may have online. With determination and regular posting, you can generate quite a significant following by building a blog.

Blog post – a post is the name given to any individual entry made to a blog. They can be long or short, and can have any one of a number of purposes, such as promoting an eBook, giving a review or an opinion of something, or perhaps giving an insight into an experience the writer has had.

Blogger – the writer who creates a blog is called a blogger. They may prefer to think of themselves primarily as a writer or an eBook writer, particularly if they are only blogging to create a buzz around their book. But they will still be thought of as a blogger by their readers.

Bonus – a bonus is any product that is given away as part of an eBook package. While the promotional material for any eBook will focus on the eBook itself, it will also mention a number of bonuses that the buyer will receive as a thank you for buying the main book.

BookSurge – this is a company which offers print on demand publishing. They are now owned by Amazon. They make POD publishing easy, quick and accessible for many authors who want to make their eBooks available in print format as well as through download (see separate entry).

Brand – a brand is a specific name that a product is known by. It may also include recognizable images that form part of that product's sales pitch. People may recognize a product simply through its logo, for example.

Business cards – these can be used to promote any type of business or product. Although they are more commonly used to represent a business, they can also be used to generate interest for a specific item; in the hope that whoever receives one of the cards will take the time to find out more about the product it advertises.

Call to action – every sales page should have a call to action. It is specifically a command that tells the reader what the writer would like them to do next. In the case of a sales page that promotes an eBook, the call to action would be for the reader to buy the eBook in question.

Car magnets – these are large sheets of magnetized, flexible material that can be attached to the side of a vehicle, or any other metal surface big enough to take them. They can be created to promote any business or product while driving in public. The idea is that you can peel them off at any time to keep them safe if you leave your vehicle unattended.

Chapter heading – this is the first part of any chapter. In order for people to understand what the chapter is going to be about, writers should always create a chapter heading for each chapter in their eBooks. It should ideally be catchy, but reveal a little of what to expect.

Chapters – the sections that go into making up a book. Splitting an eBook into chapters makes it much easier to navigate and find your way around it once you have read it. They also make it easy for someone to see what a particular book has in store.

Classified – a particular type of advert most commonly found in magazines and newspapers, but also found on certain websites. There are some websites online that specialize in providing free classifieds for people to use to advertise their products. These can get reasonable results for anyone promoting an eBook.

Click-throughs – this is the term given to the process of a person clicking on an advert or other type of link, and going through to your website (or other site). The higher the percentage of click-throughs you can get, the more successful your advert or link is deemed to be.

ClickBank – this is a website which allows you to upload and sell your eBook to a wider audience online. The main purpose of the site is to make the sales page for your eBook available to affiliates (see separate entry) that will promote your eBook for you, in return for a percentage of the profits (set by you) for any copies they sell.

Conclusion – this is the final section of the main part of any book, excluding any supplementary sections at the back, such as the index. The conclusion should wrap up the book in a satisfactory way, reiterating some of the main points while encouraging the reader to move forward from that point.

Copy – this word can have two meanings. First, the text for an eBook (or any type of book) can often be referred to as 'the copy'. The same applies to some adverts. But it can also simply refer to a single copy of a book, regardless of what format it is in.

Cover – the outside of a book, and more specifically the front of it. The cover has an important job because it must tempt people to actually go ahead and buy it. Therefore the title should be prominently displayed, and there should also be images to help seal the deal. This is applicable to eBooks as well, even though the cover will only be seen online.

Cover price – this is the selling price of a book, regardless of the format it appears in. People may occasionally receive a discount on the cover or sales price. The writer may also have to split the cover price with other people, for example if they have sold it via an affiliate.

Digital fulfillment – this refers to the process of delivering a book to a customer via online or email methods. The book itself will be an eBook (see separate entry), which may or may not be available in print form as well.

Digital fulfillment company – this is the company that provides digital fulfillment services to authors. They will take on the task of dealing with orders and sending the eBooks out to the buyers. They will usually take a cut of the cover price for each book sold.

Display – this is another form of advert, more commonly used with regards to newspaper, magazine and other printed publications, rather than for online methods of advertising.

Domain name – this is another name for a URL (see separate entry). A domain name is a unique name through which a website can be found. Some people elect to buy more than one version of their domain name, so that they have the most popular suffixes for it, such as .com and .co.uk for example.

Download – this is the term given to the method by which eBooks are usually sold. The buyer will pay for the product and will then receive a download link via an email. Upon visiting the link they can then download their eBook from the web page.

eBay – this is the most popular auction site available on which you can sell eBooks. Due to a change in the rules they now have to be supplied on disk, but this is no problem for the majority of sellers. You can also sell hard copies of your book on the site.

eBook – an eBook is a digital, downloadable version of a book. As such it has much less in the way of costs involved with it than traditionally published books do. You can keep copies of your eBook on your computer and hard drive, and simply send them to customers as and when they sell. Alternatively, you can store it online on a hidden page which is only revealed to people once they buy a copy of your book.

Editing – the process by which the first attempt at writing a complete eBook is polished and improved upon. Quite often the editing process gets better results when you have had a break in between the writing and editing processes.

Editions – some eBooks (and indeed standard books) are published initially and then re—published later on with more information in them. For example, a book may require updating at certain intervals, or the writer may want to add another couple of chapters that would be useful to the reader. These will be called first and second editions and so on.

Editors – these are people who edit books. People who write eBooks will not generally have editors, as they will go through this process themselves. Traditional publishing houses do have editors on their staff. The people who decide what material goes into magazines are also called editors.

Email signature – this is the term given to a line or two of text that is automatically put at the end of every email you send out. It was literally meant to prevent you from having to re—type your name at the end of every email, but marketers and writers use it to promote their latest offering, eBook or website.

Examples – in the context of eBooks, examples are used to make certain points easier for the reader to understand. They are highly important, particularly when the writer wants to get across a certain point that they personally believe in.

FAQ – this is short for frequently asked questions, and it appears on many websites. It is a particularly important section of a website as it will answer many of the most common questions received by the staff there. It also provides a quick way to understand the nature of a site.

First draft – this is the term given to the first complete attempt at writing a book or article of any kind. Once the basic work is done, the writer can then set about editing it to make sure it all makes sense and runs as smoothly as possible.

Flyers – these are small pieces of paper which have adverts printed on them, for the main purpose of delivering door to door. They may also be distributed in newspapers or magazines, or given out by hand in certain situations.

Forum – a forum is an online discussion website that allows people to talk about different topics. Most forums have a specific area of interest, and they allow people to have a signature line underneath every post they make. This can be used to promote your own website if the rules of the forum allow it.

Freebie – this term is sometimes used interchangeably with the word 'bonus' when referring to the additional products which come with an eBook. However, an eBook itself can also be called a freebie if it is given away without charge. This sometimes happens as a way to build an audience and a mailing list of people who will be interested in future books.

Graphic – the term given to a design which can be used as an eBook cover. A graphic is more specifically an artistic drawing or image, rather than a photograph.

Hard copy – a hard copy is a book which exists in print format, rather than as an eBook. An eBook can be transferred into print format as well however, and in this case it would be in hard copy too.

HTML – this stands for hyper text mark—up language. It is the language which creates the layout of a website, although it is gradually being superseded to some extent by cascading style sheets, or CSS. If you know a little bit of html, you will be able to do more when it comes to building Squidoo pages (see separate entry) and other similar tasks.

Inbound links – these are links coming from another website and pointing towards your own. In terms of search engine optimization importance they are ranked quite highly. This is because the more inbound links your website has, the more important it is thought to be, as other websites deem it necessary to link to yours.

Information products – this is the catch all term given to any type of product which imparts information to the reader. So for example, we could include eBooks in this description, as well as newsletters, reports and even some kinds of software. Provided the buyer gets information, then they have bought an information product.

Internet marketing – this is the term given to promoting and selling items or services over the internet. Internet marketing is very different from promoting items offline. It may happen through advertising on other websites as well as through having your own site.

Introduction – the first section of a book, before the main bulk of the chapters begin. As such, the introduction should provide an insight into what the reader can expect from the book as a whole and what they will learn as a result of reading it.

ISBN number – ISBN stands for international standard book number. Any book that has one will be much easier to search for online or via any bookseller, since the system is a universal one that is used in many countries. It is also necessary to have one if you want to sell your books in bookstores and on sites like Amazon.

Keyword density – this refers to the number of times (given as a percentage) that a particular word appears on a page or in a specific document. So for example, if your web page has 500 words in it and the keyword 'eBook' appears in it 12 times, then it will have a keyword density of 2.4%. To work out the keyword density, the number of times the keyword appears is divided by the total number of words and then multiplied by 100.

Keyword tool – this is a tool which helps you to find appropriate and popular keywords to use when constructing a web page, finding the topic for a new eBook, or writing a sales letter. You may start with a basic keyword, and it will suggest lots of others in the same area that people have looked up using the search engines.

Lens – a lens is the name given to a free web page created with the help of the website Squidoo. A lens can be an excellent way of promoting an eBook or any other product, as Squidoo allows its users to promote most things with the help of its site, as well as earning money at the same time.

Lightning Source – this is a print on demand publisher that can be used by eBook writers to make their eBook available as a hard copy through such outlets as Amazon. Using a company like this can vastly increase the number of books you will sell.

Lineage ad – this is another name for a classified advert. It is so called because the ads appear in lines, rather than in a display or boxed format.

Lulu – Lulu is a website which offers publishing facilities to all authors. There are no upfront charges for their services as they take a commission from each book sold instead. They can publish eBooks for authors, and also operate as print on demand publishers.

Mailing list – many authors create a mailing list by giving away an eBook for free, in exchange for the name and email address of the person requesting it. They may also create a list by getting people to opt into it when they buy an eBook from them. This gives them a ready made audience to write and sell the next eBook to.

Market – your market is the specific group of people you promote your eBook (or other product) to. Depending on the subject of your book, your market could be big or small, and this is something that should be borne in mind when you are looking for topics for new eBooks, as it could affect the potential profit in a subject.

Mini-site –term that is often given to the website that you will sell your eBook on. The best results are obtained when a single site is given over to one specific book. So rather than having a home page and lots of other pages as well, there will be a long sales letter (which is usually the home-page), privacy policy, disclaimer, and a contact us.

Misspellings – these are sometimes used in the copy for websites, in order to catch surfers who are looking for the information you have, but spell certain words wrong when they are searching for it. A keyword tool (see separate entry) can be used to find such misspellings.

Modules – these are the separate components of lenses created on Squidoo. There are dozens of modules to choose from, and each one has a different purpose. As such the number of variations you could have in the lenses is almost infinite, as there is no limit on the length of a lens.

Niches – niches are specific areas of interest that capture the attention of a specific audience. Although a niche will target less people, it is actually far easier to sell to a niche audience than it is to sell to a large audience which represents a wide cross section of society. You may also experience sub—niches, which drill down into a main niche to tackle certain dedicated areas of it.

Optimized results – this is the term given to search engine results, when they are searched for in inverted commas. When you search for a particular term, the search engines will look for any web page that has any combination of the words you look for. But if you put that search term in inverted commas it will narrow down the results to include only those ones that contains those specific words in that exact order.

PayPal – this is one of the internet's biggest payment processors. It is most commonly associated with the auction site eBay, but it can also be used as a payment processor on many other websites. They provide all the things you need to do this, including payment buttons and logos for use on your website.

PDF format – PDF stands for portable document format, and it is the type of file most often used when publishing eBooks. When an eBook is in PDF format, it can easily be opened and read by other people, mainly because the software to do so is already installed on many computers. If they do not have it, it can be obtained free of charge and installed by the user very easily in a matter of seconds.

Pitch page – a pitch page is simply another name for a sales page. Some websites prefer to call the site where an eBook or other product is promoted on a single page as a pitch page, since it offers a sales pitch for the product concerned.

Post – with regard to forums, a post is a single entry in a forum thread (see separate entry). A post may be an answer to a post someone else has already made, or it may start a whole new topic of conversation. Your signature can be added to each post you make automatically.

Print on demand (POD) – print on demand is the new way of publishing books without having a huge outlay up front that you hope you can get back through the cost of selling books. Print on demand quite simply means that as each copy is ordered; it will be printed individually and sent straight out to the customer.

Print run – this is the term given to a single job performed by a printer. For example, if you were to order a hundred copies of your latest book to be printed in advance of the publication date, that would be called a print run. A book may have one or more print runs depending on its popularity. If it is published via print on demand methods, then each print run will consist of a single copy.

Professional writer – this refers to someone who writes for a living, or who at least writes regularly for various markets and has been published as a result. They may also be known as an author, if they have written books of any description, whether these are self published or published by a main publishing house.

Profile – this is the term given to the page you will have on sites such as Squidoo, that gives people an idea of who you are and what you do. It is important to fill this in and make it as interesting as possible, as it can lead to more book sales. There is usually a specific place to put your website address so more people can find you.

PS – a powerful technique used in sales pages. Many people will scroll to the bottom of the page to see what the price is, so if you have at least one PS there which mentions the best part of buying the product, you will stand a better chance of making a sale.

Publication – this can mean two things. A magazine or newspaper is often referred to as a publication. But it can also mean the publication – or release – of a book or eBook, i.e. the date on which it is available to buy.

Reports – shorter information products are often referred to as reports. They can be given away free with an eBook, or sold individually at a lower price.

Resource box – this is the small paragraph of text that appears at the end of every article submitted to and published on an article directory. This is the one place you can advertise your website or eBook, as you cannot promote anything within the article itself.

Retail price – this is another term for the cover price of a book. It may be reduced either to attract more sales or to get rid of outstanding stock to make way for new items.

Rewrites – this usually refers to the editing process of a book. A rewrite will enable the author to turn out a better quality book than if they had simply published the first attempt. However, rewrites can also refer to later editions of a book.

Sales letter – this is another term that is sometimes used to describe the website that an eBook is sold from. It is more often used, however, to describe a sales pitch that is actually sent through the mail.

Sans serif – this is a kind of typeface that is commonly used for eBooks that will be read on screen. This is because it does not have curly ends to the letters, which can make them harder to read online.

Screenshots – a screenshot is a picture of a portion of a website. They are commonly used in eBooks to help illustrate certain points or instructions, as they can show the reader exactly what they should be looking at when they follow a specific task. They also help to break up the text.

Search engines – these help you to find your way around the internet and search for websites on specific subjects. Google and Yahoo are perhaps the two most well known search engines around today.

Search facility – this is a facility provided on many websites that allows you to search for information on that particular site. It is also present on all keyword tools (see separate entry) as it lets you search for relevant and related keywords to the one you have in mind to begin with.

Self publish – this is the process of publishing an eBook, paperback or hardback book yourself, as opposed to going through a traditional publisher to do it. It has many benefits, but it can also be more difficult in a way as you are responsible for performing all the most important roles yourself.

Selling price – this is the cover price of the book. When you are self publishing, you set this price yourself, instead of relying on the publisher to set it for you.

SEO – this is short for search engine optimization. It refers to the process of tweaking your website so that it is made visible to the search engines. By optimizing your website, you can also make your site visible to more people by including specific keywords that are relevant to the subject of your site.

Serif – this is a kind of typeface that isn't often used online. This is because the letters in serif typefaces are curly at the ends, as opposed to finishing with no elaborate shapes at all. As a result, they aren't as easy to read on a computer screen.

Signed copies – some authors offer to sign copies of their books to make them more attractive to potential buyers. They will usually only contain a brief and generic greeting, and often only contain the signature itself. They may also have a 'signed by author' sticker on the outside to encourage more interest.

Social bookmarking – a social bookmarking site is a website that allows users to bookmark websites they like online, instead of bookmarking them on their computer. By doing this, they can always get access to them, no matter what computer they are on, as well as sharing them with others. For anyone selling online, it is beneficial to bookmark and share all your websites and articles that lead to them.

Social networking – these sites allow you to get connected with other like minded people, with the idea that they may become future customers. While a lot of people use the sites purely for socializing online, many also use them to connect with their audience when selling eBooks or other products.

Software – an item of software is something that you can purchase and install on your computer. It will help you to perform a certain action or function, such as creating eBook formats that you wouldn't be able to do otherwise.

Spamming – this is the practice of sending unsolicited email or requests to people. Spamming is strictly prohibited and you can be fined if you are found to be doing it. Posting lots of similar comments in order to promote yourself on forums and other similar websites is also known as spamming.

Specialist magazine – this refers to a magazine that focuses on a specific hobby or interest. Rather than appealing to a mass market, it will concentrate on a smaller group of people.

Squidoo – this is a website which allows its users to join for free and build as many separate web pages as they wish. Many eBook sellers and affiliates use it to help promote sales and books.

Sub—domain – this is an extension of a main domain. If you join a website and receive a free web page from it, then it will usually be in the form of a sub—domain. An example would be www.maindomain.com/subdomain.

Sweetening the deal – this is the process that is used to make it more likely that more people will buy whatever it is you are selling. For example, you may offer additional products as well as the main one when you are selling an eBook. These may be well in excess of the value of the main product.

Tags – tags are commonly used on Squidoo (see separate entry). They are used to help identify that a specific page is about a specific subject, thus making it easier to find by other people during a search.

Testimonials – these help to sell products. A testimonial is usually a paragraph or two written by a previous customer, saying how the product has helped them and why they are glad they bought it.

Text – this is another word for the writing that makes up an eBook or web page. The text refers specifically to the words, rather than including any images as well.

Thread – a thread is the term given to a new subject being talked about on a forum. There may be lots of separate forum posts in a single thread.

Title – the title is what attracts people to an eBook, or any other kind of information product. As such it should pull people in instantly, making them want to know more. The title is extremely important.

Traffic – the number of people who visit your website are collectively known as traffic. Put simply, the more traffic you can get, the better your chances are of making more sales. Ideally the traffic will come from more than one source as well.

Typeface – this is the choice of type you use for presenting your book. For example, Verdana is a typeface and so is Times New Roman. There are hundreds to choose from, but some are habitually used much more often than others.

URL – this stands for uniform resource locator. It is basically another name for a domain, and it indicates where a particular website can be found, via its unique address on the web.

Volume – this refers to a copy of a book, more usually in hard copy rather than as an eBook. A particular book may appear in more than one volume if it is too big to be published as a single one.

Website address – this is also known as a URL. This is the address at which a particular website can be found on the internet.

Wordtracker – this is a tool which can be used for free to find keywords to use for a particular product. They also have a more complex paid service which gives more features and advantages over the free one.

Writer's block – some writers will suffer from this now and again. Writer's block is the term given to the situation where you cannot write, no matter what you try and do.

Resources

These are a selection of resources which you may find helpful when you are writing your own eBook. They are provided in sections where appropriate.

Keyword tools:

- Google AdWords Tool – this will help you with keywords
  https://adwords.google.com/select/KeywordToolExternal
- Wordtracker – another free keyword tool generator
  http://freekeywords.wordtracker.com
- GTrends – another free service from Wordtracker
  http://freekeywords.wordtracker.com/gtrends

Useful sites for writing and preparing for publication:

- ISBN International – the organization which will tell you where you should apply for an ISBN number in your own country
  http://www.isbn—international.org/index.html
- SXC – website for free picture use
  http://www.sxc.hu
- Adobe Acrobat – for generating PDF copies of your eBook
  http://www.adobe.com
- PayPal – for opening an account and generating pay buttons on your website
  www.paypal.com
- Elance – just in case you need help in writing or editing your eBook
  http://www.elance.com

Useful sites for selling your eBook:

- Amazon – the biggest and the best online bookseller
  www.amazon.com

- Lulu – a print on demand publisher that also accepts eBooks
  http://www.lulu.com
- BookSurge – another print on demand publisher
  http://www.booksurge.com
- Lightning Source—giant print on demand service provider to publishing companies
  http://www.lightningsource.com
  http://www.lightningsource.co.uk
- ClickBank – if you want an army of affiliates selling your eBook for you
  www.clickbank.com
- Bookhitch – for listing your eBook once it is published, free of charge
  http://www.bookhitch.com
- eBooks Café – for listing your eBook for free
  http://www.ebookscafe.writergazette.com
- eBook 2 U – again, another free listing site
  http://www.ebook2u.com

Useful sites for promoting your eBook:

- Sites for distributing press releases online free of charge
  http://www.free—press—release.com
  http://www.freepressreleases.co.uk
  http://www.prlog.org
- Squidoo – for building free web pages to promote your eBook
  http://www.squidoo.com
- SquidU – if you need help on Squidoo
  http://www.squidu.com/
- EZHtml – for getting to grips with html for web pages
  http://www.ezhtml.net
- UWC Blog Network – if you want a free blog that you want to promote your eBook on http://uwcblog.com

- Vistaprint – often has free offers for business cards and so on
  http://www.vistaprint.com
- Article directories – for writing and distributing articles to help promote your eBook (via the resource box)
  http://www.articledashboard.com
  http://www.articlegold.com
  http://www.ezinearticles.com
  http://www.goarticles.com
  http://www.ideamarketers.com
  http://www.searchwarp.com
- Social networking sites – for raising your profile and driving traffic to your eBook website
  http://www.myspace.com
  http://www.facebook.com
  http://twitter.com
  http://www.bebo.com
  http://www.linkedin.com (business focus)
- Social bookmarking sites – for sharing your websites and articles with others!
  http://www.digg.com
  http://del.icio.us
  http://www.technorati.com
  http://www.stumbleupon.com
  http://www.reddit.com

Index